Buried New Hampshire

Graveyards Have Stories to Tell

—VOLUME II—

RICK DAVIDSON AND BILL THOMPSON

AMERICA
THROUGH
TIME

America Through Time®
An imprint of Sutton Publishing Inc
www.through-time.com

First published 2025
Copyright © Rick Davidson and Bill Thompson 2025

ISBN 978-1-63499-568-9

Typeset in 10pt on 13pt Sabon
Printed and bound in the United States of America

Preface

Buried New Hampshire is a collection of stories and photographs of grave sites and cemeteries in New Hampshire. We have spent over a year traveling throughout the state, searching out locations and researching the stories and legends behind the places we visited. Our journey was guided by a deep respect for the deceased, and we have written about many historical figures, some of whom are well-known and others who have fallen into obscurity. We discovered and learned about politicians, entertainers, artists, authors, murder victims, movers and shakers, occasional ghosts, and enslaved people. As New Hampshire natives, many were unknown to us beforehand.

In some cases, we had to make decisions about historical discrepancies; in others, we had to rely on local lore. We have referenced what we believe to be reliable sources. We aim to share what we have learned with the reader and stimulate your curiosity and imagination. We have tried to be historically accurate and, at the same time, entertaining. We have included our observations as well as those of others. The art and iconology of gravestones is a subject unto itself, and in some cases, we have discussed this; many fine publications cover this topic in far greater detail. The table of contents provides you with the names of the cemeteries. However, we did not intend to provide detailed directions to these locations, and in some cases, we have left out details to protect private property.

From the outset, we realized that the number of stories we might tell far outnumbered what we could include in one book. So, as it turns out, *Buried New Hampshire* has been published in two volumes. This is volume two. It contains an equal number of interesting "buried" personalities and stories as the first volume. It can stand independently; the stories are as compelling as those in volume one. It has been a fun year; we hope you, the reader, enjoy this book as much as we did in photographing and writing it.

Rick Davidson and Bill Thompson

CONTENTS

1
EARLY CEMETERIES AND MARKERS OF NEW HAMPSHIRE

Point of Graves, Portsmouth

Point of Graves is the oldest cemetery in the City of Portsmouth and perhaps the second oldest in the state. It is thought that the site was used as a burial ground as early as 1650, although it was not recognized as an official cemetery until 1671, when Captain John Pickering gave the town a half-acre of land for the purpose. The good captain continued to graze livestock on the land even after signing over the land; thus, many earlier stones were destroyed. This was not an uncommon practice, and the Cotton Cemetery in Portsmouth was also used as pasture. The earliest known stone in Point of Graves is dated 1682. For the record, Pine Grove Cemetery in Hampton dates to 1654 and lays claim to being the second oldest burial ground in the state; Odiorne Point, in Rye, being the first.

Many of Portsmouth's first "well-to-do" are buried at Point of Graves, including the Wentworth and the Vaughan families. This accounts for why there are so many beautiful carved stones in the cemetery. Gravestones were expensive in colonial times, and most of the markers at Point of Graves were shipped from Boston. Point of Graves is of special interest to scholars of colonial iconography and funerary imagery. Many of the stones are signed by the noted gravestone carvers of the Boston area. There are examples by William Mumford, Nathaniel Emmes, John Homer, and the carver known by the initials "J. N." Other carvers include Caleb and Nathaniel Lamson of Charlestown, James Foster of Dorchester, and John Hartshorne and Joseph Mullicken, both of Haverhill. Many of these early markers are adorned with images of skulls and winged death heads, which were popular in colonial times.

Like many old cemeteries, Point of Graves is said to be haunted. One legend is that the Vaughan tomb glows at night. The tomb does have an interesting story. In August 1884, the tomb was opened, and twenty-eight bodies were found to have been buried there. The youngest is a two-month-old infant. The existing tomb is a marble replica of the original stone that was on the ground. With all those folks stuffed into one tomb, one can see why there might be some discord.

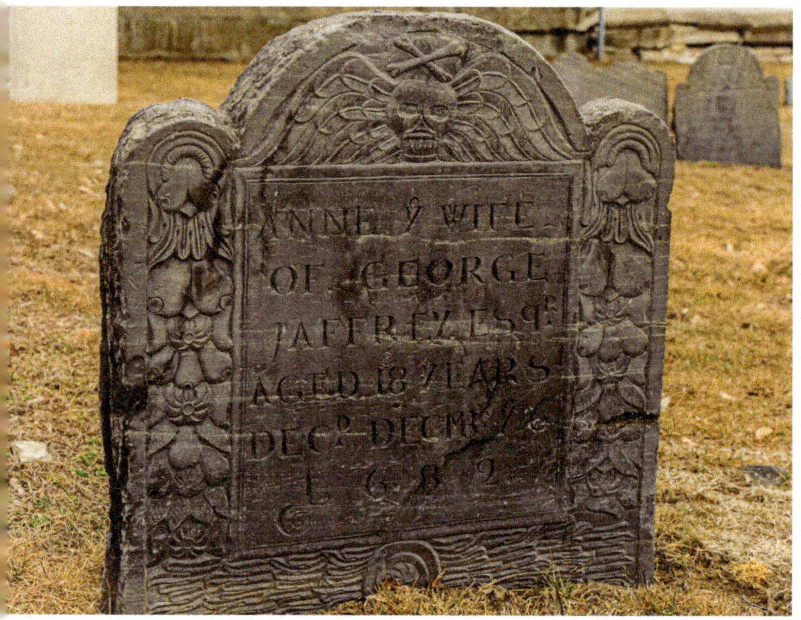

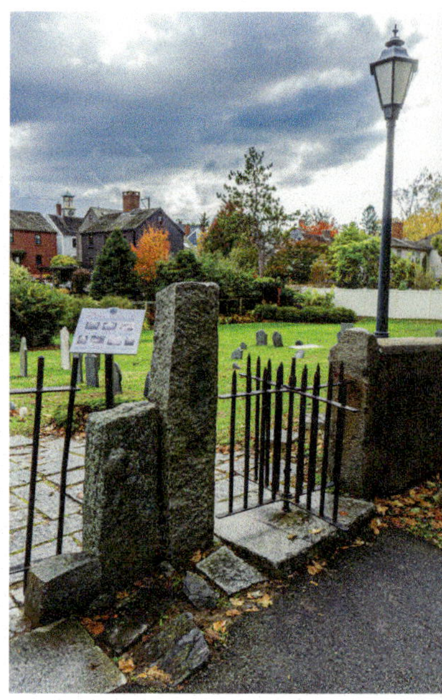

Above left: The oldest grave.

Above right: Point of Graves gate.

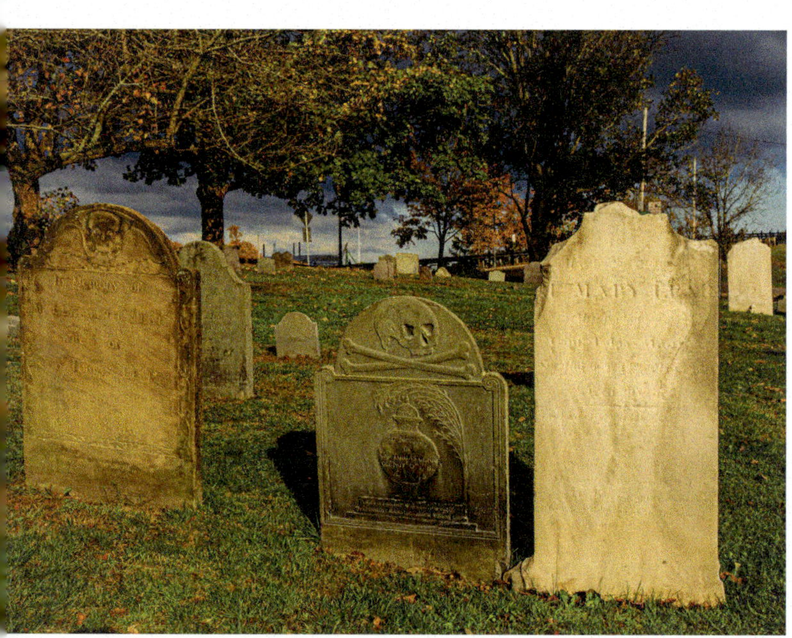

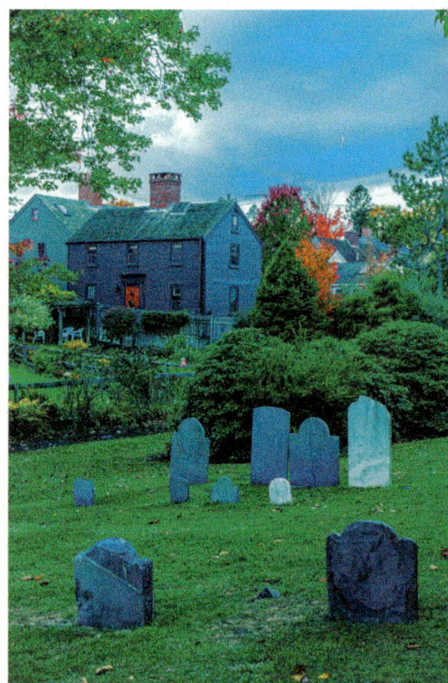

Above left: Example of skull engraving.

Above right: Cemetery looking to Strawberry Bank.

North Cemetery, Portsmouth

North Cemetery is the burial ground of the "who's who" of Revolutionary Portsmouth. It is the second oldest cemetery in Portsmouth. The first burials date to 1751; however, it was not until 1753 that the city purchased the land from Colonel John Hart, the commander of the New Hampshire Regiment at Louisburg, who is also interned in North Cemetery. Some of the many Revolutionary-era luminaires are buried here. John Langdon, governor of New Hampshire and signer of the Constitution; his brother, Woodbury Langdon, also a delegate to the Continental Congress; William Whipple, signer of the Declaration of Independence and general in the Continental Army; Prince Whipple, the slave of William; and Captain Thomas Thompson, commander of the *Raleigh*, the same ship depicted on the Seal of New Hampshire are all buried in North Cemetery. We have covered many of these individuals in other chapters.

The cemetery is located on Maplewood Ave, bordered by Union Cemetery. When established, it was undoubtedly a much more tranquil location. However, after 200 years of urban expansion, it is situated in a busy commercial area today. Despite this, it has its own beauty, especially in the fall. The heroes of the American Revolution who rest in North Cemetery are all but forgotten compared to those from other states.

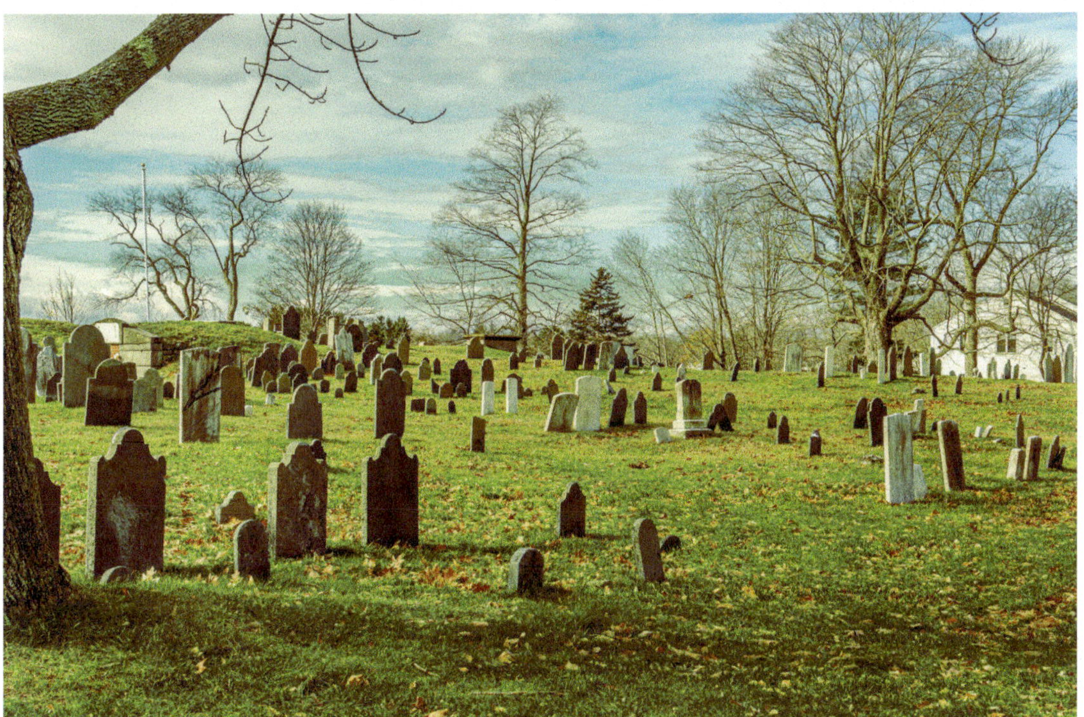

North Cemetery view.

Frost Cemetery, New Castle

The lovely little Frost Cemetery can be found directly across from the New Castle Town Hall on NH Route 1B. This was the private burial ground of the Frost and Bell families, dating to the early 1700s. Presumed to be the earliest grave is that of Captain John Holcomb, who died in 1721. Holcomb captained the merchant ship *Sarah* and traded between Barbados and Portsmouth. Honorable John Frost Esq., another sea captain and wealthy merchant of New Castle, is also buried here. There are other notable men interned in the Frost Cemetery; however, it is the grave of Abigail Frost, the daughter of John, whom students of iconography come to visit. Abigail's stone bears a striking relief sculpture of a beautiful young woman, presumably that of her. Abigail died on June 30, 1742, at the age of twenty-three. Aside from the beauty of the carving, it represents the evolution of gravestone carvings from winged skulls and images of soul cherubs to more realistic carvings of the deceased.

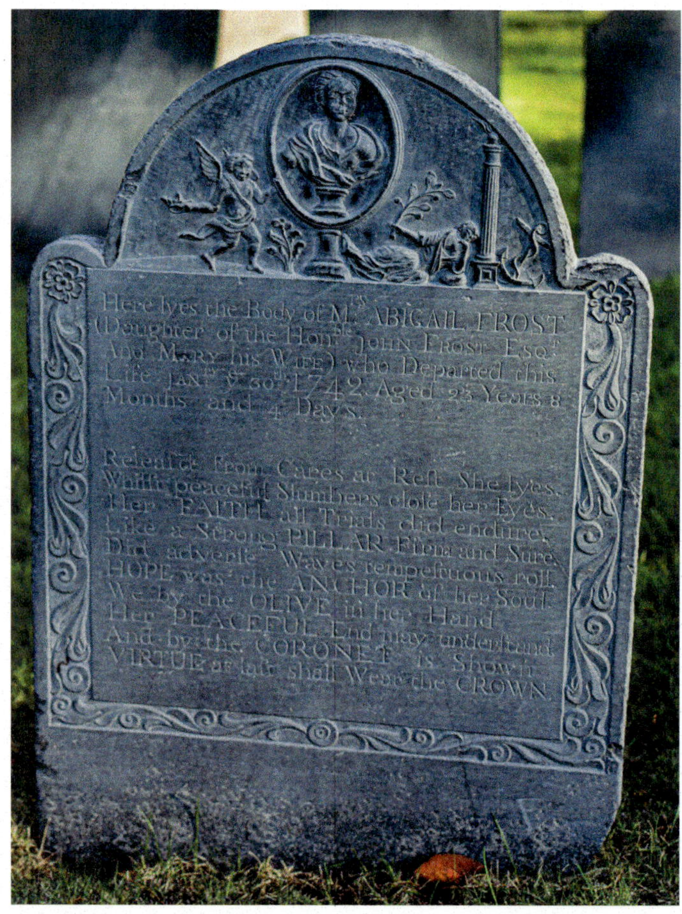

Grave of Abigail Frost.

South Cemetery, Portsmouth

South Cemetery could be the prettiest cemetery in New Hampshire. This is a bold statement to make, as there are many beautiful cemeteries in the Granite State. This is especially true in the fall when it is ablaze with autumn color. The residents of Portsmouth are fond of walking or jogging through the park-like cemetery, no matter what time of year.

South Cemetery combines five separate cemeteries: Cotton, Elmwood, Harmony Grove, Proprietor's Burial Ground, and Sagamore. The oldest is Cotton Cemetery. In 1721, William Cotton was given a portion of land to clear to be used for cattle grazing and a training ground. On this land, Cotton established a family cemetery. The Elmwood portion was also a family plot. Over time, various church groups came to own sections of the cemetery. In 1825, the Trustees of the South Church Charitable Fund laid out the first private cemetery in Portsmouth, the Proprietors Burial Ground. In 1847, Harmony Grove was laid out, and in 1871, Sagamore Cemetery was added. For a while, the newer sections were called the Auburn

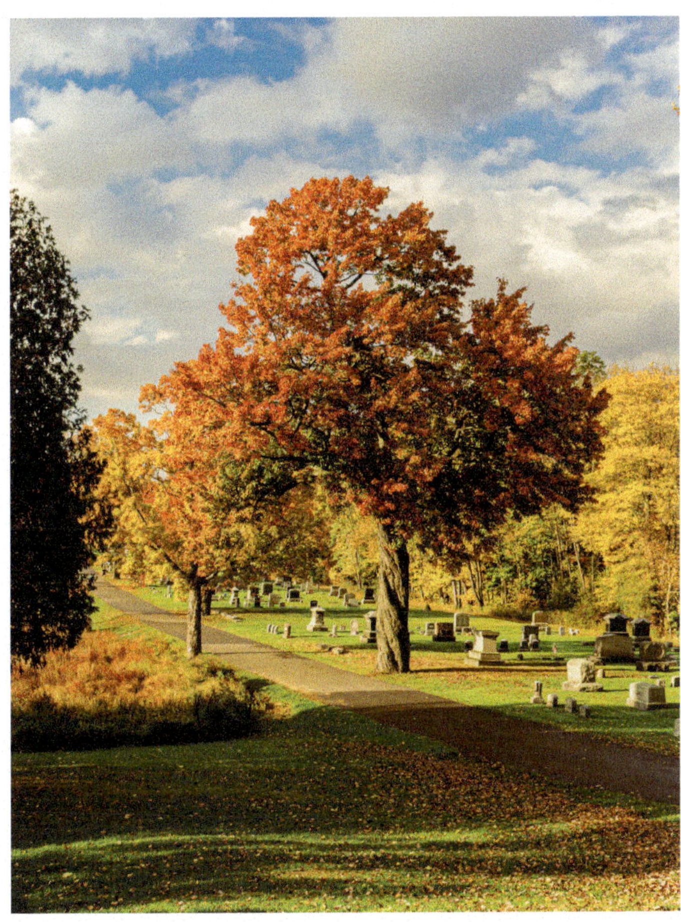

View of South Cemetery.

Cemetery due to the adjacent Auburn Street. The street was later renamed, and the name fell into disuse. Harmony Grove and Proprietors are still privately owned by the Griffin family.

Many famous and infamous people are buried in South Cemetery, many of whom we have included in other chapters. Perhaps the most poignant story is that of Ruth Blay, the last woman hanged in New Hampshire. Her grave is unmarked, presumably in the area near the Cotton Cemetery where the gallows stood. Another tragic story is that of Anethe Mater and Karen Christensen, the victims of the Smuttynose Murders. The sisters are buried in the Harmony Grove section. One of the most opulent monuments is that of Jack Jones, the local brewer and robber baron. Two of Portsmouth's most famous brothel owners, Mary Baker and Alta Roberts, are buried in the Sagamore section.

South Cemetery, of course, has its fair share of ghostly tales. Ruth Blay is said to be seen and heard on occasion. One interesting story is that of the "Glowing Gravestone." There is said to be a stone that glows without the aid of passing cars or moonlight. It has become a favorite destination for would-be ghost hunters and students from UNH.

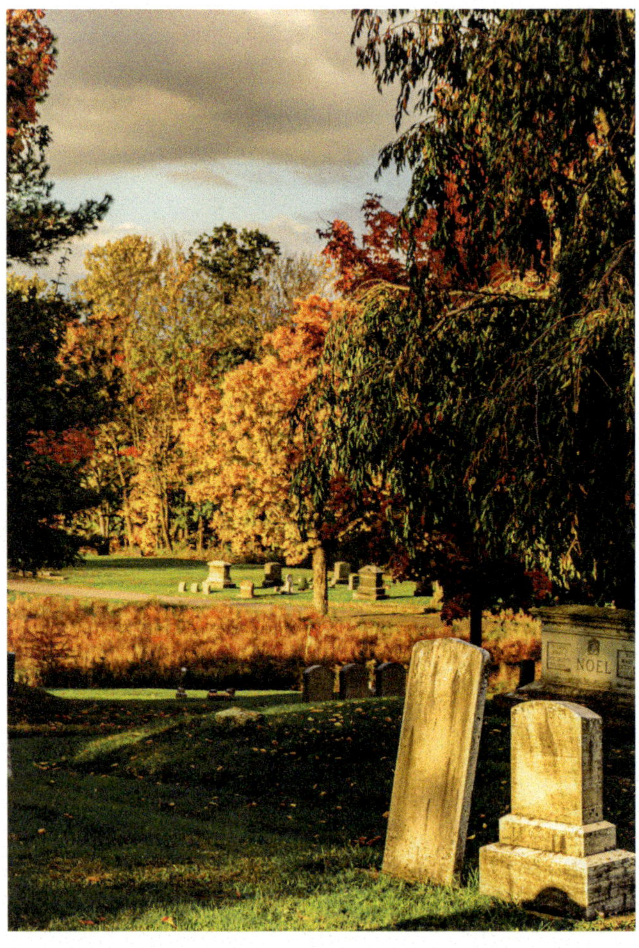

View of South Cemetery.

Pine Grove Cemetery and Ring Swamp Cemetery, Hampton

Hampton is one of the four original townships in New Hampshire. The General Court of Massachusetts granted Richard Drummer and John Spencer of Newburyport the right to establish a settlement known as Winnacunnet Plantation in 1636. Winnacunnet in Abenaki translates to pleasant pines and is the current name of the local high school. The first settlers, led by the Reverend Stephen Bachiler, arrived in 1638. Bachiler, who had once preached in Hampton, England, renamed the town Hampton. A triangular-shaped common, across from the Tuck Museum, on Winnncunnet Road is the site of the original meeting house. Just down the road, from the common and across from Mill Road, is Pine Grove Cemetery, established in 1654 and one of the earliest cemeteries in New Hampshire.

Pine Grove is a lovely little cemetery surrounded by a stone wall with a white picket gate. It is aptly named as it contains some magnificent pine trees. Over the centuries, many of the early stones have disappeared into the sandy soil, some reemerging from time to time. One of the more interesting is a plaque in memory of Edward Grove. King Charles II appointed a new governor to the Providence of New Hampshire, Edward Cranfield. Cranfield was not a popular fellow, and he began raising taxes. Grove and a lot of other people took issue. Grove managed to distinguish himself by riding from Hampton to Exeter shouting "Liberty and Reformation," thus earning a quick trip to the goal and an all-expense trip back to England to be tried and hanged for treason. He spent three years in the Tower of London, awaiting his fate. Fortunately for Grove, King Charles died, and the new king, Edward II, pardoned Grove, and he returned to Hampton. What came to be called "Grove's Rebellion" was an early indicator of the American Revolution. Grove passed away in 1692 and is buried in Pine Grove Cemetery.

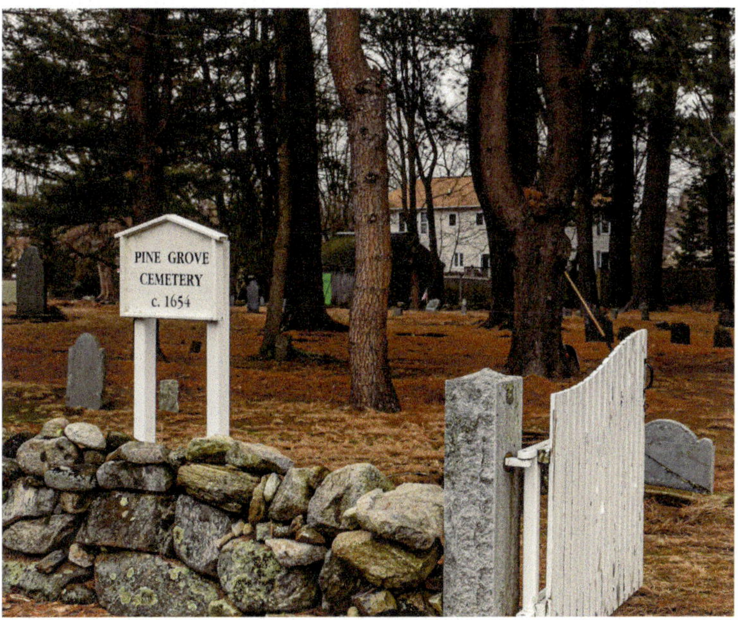

Pine Grove gate.

Ring Swamp Cemetery

A lesser-known cemetery in Hampton is Ring Swamp Cemetery. Founded in 1799, it is the town's second public cemetery. It is almost surrounded by the Winnicunnet High School campus. The entrance is off High Street. The unusual and beautiful gate is attributed to a local blacksmith named Enoch Young. It is made of wrought iron and depicts a swan. A great many of those interned are veterans of the American Revolutionary War. However, the one stone that stands out is that of Lucy G. Haselton. Situated in the middle of the cemetery, the stone is easily visible; made of marble, it is strikingly white. What sets it apart is that one side has a beautifully carved hand pointing down. The stone was lovingly placed by her family, so we doubt very much that they thought their daughter was going to hell. The hand is grasping a garland of flowers and points to a plaque inscribed "LUCY."

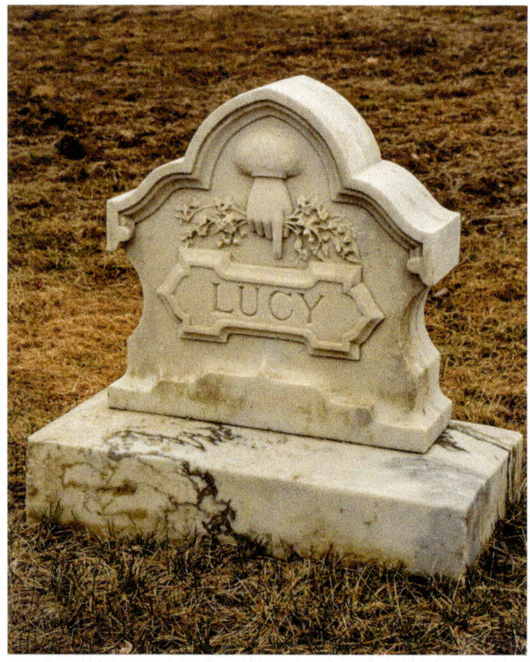

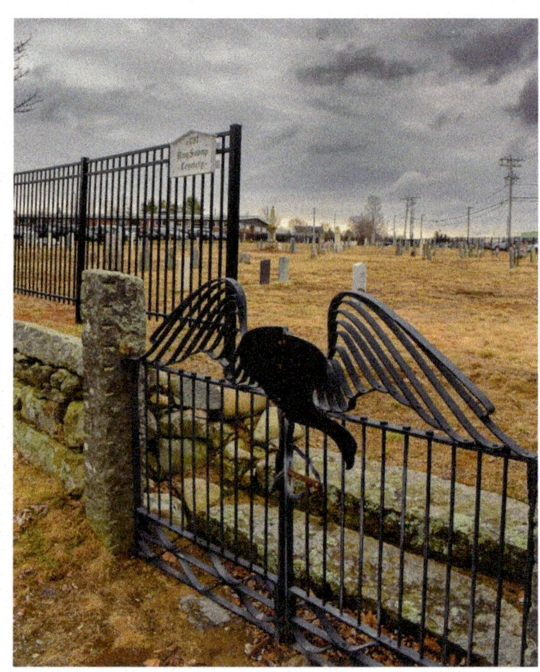

Above left: Lucy in Ring Swamp Cemetery.

Above right: Ring Swamp gate.

Opposite left: Old Road Cemetery.

Opposite right: Old Road Cemetery.

Peterborough Old Street Road (East Hill) Cemetery, Est. 1754

The people of Peterborough believe that *Our Town*, the famous play by Thornton Wilder about Grover's Corners, is based on their town. Wilder wrote *Our Town* while in residence at the MacDowell Artist Colony in Peterborough. "Grover's Corners" is very likely named after the intersection of Grove Street and Main Street. Well-known actor James Whitmore played the stage manager in that theater for many years. Recently, the part was played by North Conway native and Emmy Award winner Gordan Clapp. The play's first production at the Peterborough Players Theater was in 1940, and Thornton Wilder served as a consultant.

In the town cemetery in Act III, we learn about the fate of some citizens of Grover's Corners since we last saw them at George and Emily's wedding. Most shocking is when we know of the death of Emily, who died while giving birth. Emily joins the dead. Emily's grave is not in East Hill Cemetery, but the remains of many of the once-living nonfictional residents are.

One of the most well-known graves contains the remnants of William Diamond, the drummer boy of the Battle of Lexington. There are other Revolutionary War soldiers interred there. Every person has a story. The set of *Our Town* is generally minimal. Chairs are sometimes used to represent the cemetery. There is something about this play that invites all of us to imagine our own hometowns and to trigger memories of our personal pasts. Now that I have visited Old Street Road Cemetery, I somehow feel the presence there of the fictional citizens of "Grover's Corners" resting along with those once very much alive people who populated Peterborough and its environs. I see Emily hanging back only to realize we should treasure every moment of life. Do we do that while we are alive? According to the stage manager, we don't.

> We all know that something is eternal. And it ain't houses and it ain't names, and it ain't earth, and it ain't even the stars … everybody knows in their bones that something is eternal and that something has to do with human beings.

> Thornton Wilder
> *Our Town*

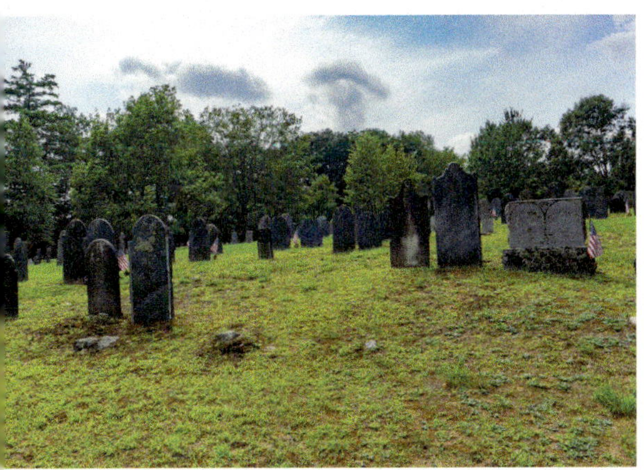

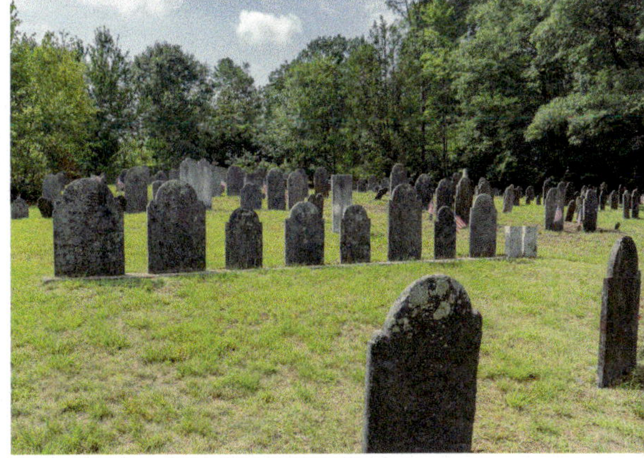

Pine Grove Cemetery, Manchester, Est. 1851

Bill and I visited the Pine Grove Cemetery on a beautiful early fall day. This cemetery is the final resting place of many Manchester mayors and has more mausoleums than any other cemetery we have visited. There are eighteen of them. Guided by cemetery employees, we found Frank Pierce Carpenter (1845–1938), an influential entrepreneur, philanthropist, and president of Amoskeag Manufacturing Company, who was involved with banks, insurance, and the Boston and Maine Railroad. He was chairperson of the commission for the erection of the statue of Franklin Pierce. He donated the Carpenter Library in Manchester in memory of his wife, Elenor R. Blood Carpenter. It is one of the most impressive libraries in New Hampshire. His heirs later turned over their Queen Anne-style home to the Red Cross.

Frank and Elenor's daughter, Mary Elizabeth Carpenter, married the boy next door, Charles Bartlett Manning (1873–1924). Charles was an engineer who studied at Harvard and MIT, but tragedy struck. A train pulling Henry Ford's private railroad car hit and killed outdoorsmen Charles and his brothers, Robert and Francis, while hiking along a railroad track in Grafton. Many mourned the loss of the Manning boys. Our guides mentioned that one of the Mannings was an entertainer. I could find no evidence of this. There is a Frank Manning buried at the Manning Memorial, but he is not Frank Manning, the swing dancer.

Next, we visited Alonzo Elliot (1891–1964), who wrote "There's a Long Trail Winding" with his friend Stoddard King at Yale. Created on a whim, this became one of the most popular songs of World War I:

> *There's a long, long trail a-winding*
> *Into the land of my dreams,*
> *Where the nightingales are singing*
> *And the white moon beams.*
> *There's a long, long night of waiting*
> *Until my dreams all come true;*
> *Till the day when I'll be going down*
> *That long, long trail with you.*

One could picture a soldier imagining his return home to a loved one.

After visiting Alonzo, we visited another entertainer, Betty George (1926–1997), known as the Greek Goddess of song. She was a Decca and CBS recording artist who sang with such big bands as Glenn Miller, Artie Shaw, Glen Gray, Xavier Coughart, and Tommy Dorsey. She worked with Milton Berle for over sixteen years. She appeared on Broadway in *Anchors Aweigh*, *As the Girls Go*, and *Heaven on Earth*. Quite a career.

Nehemiah S. Bean (1818–1896) apprenticed with Shakers in Canterbury and went on to create and build steam fire engines. Even though Bean and local mechanic Thomas Scott had never seen such a machine, they built the Amoskeag #1, which could shoot water upwards of 155 feet. Amoskeag Steam fire engines revolutionized firefighting.

Civil War-era Doctors Esther Hill Hawkes and her husband are buried in Pine Grove Cemetery. More on them can be found elsewhere in this book.

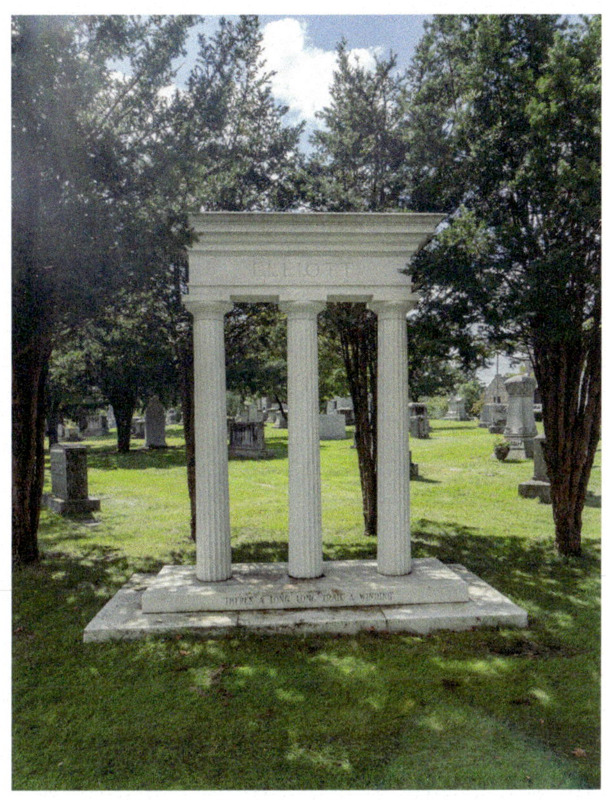

Alonzo Elliot, musician.

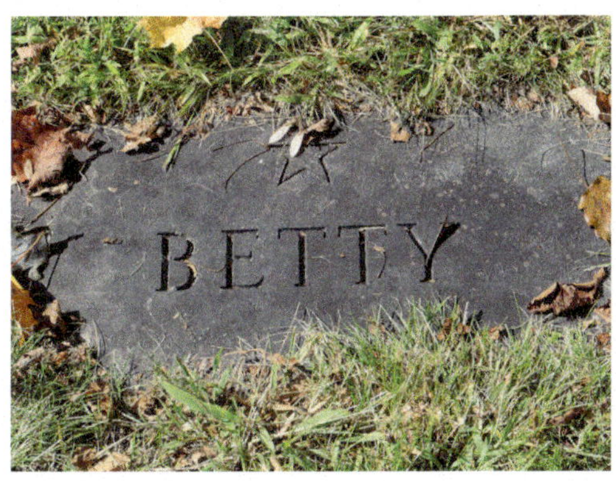

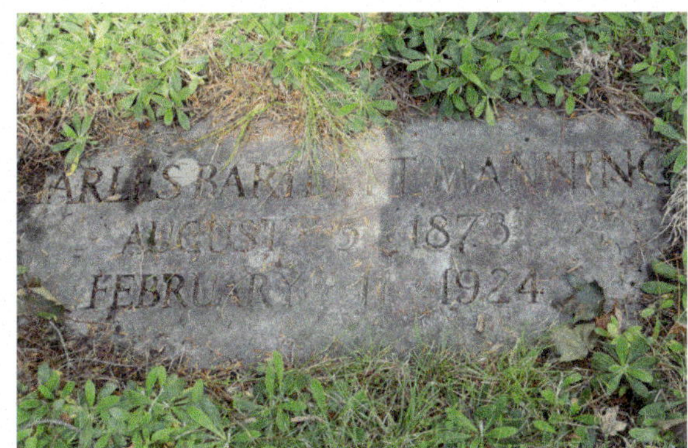

Above left: Betty George, actress.

Above right: Charles Manning, accident victim.

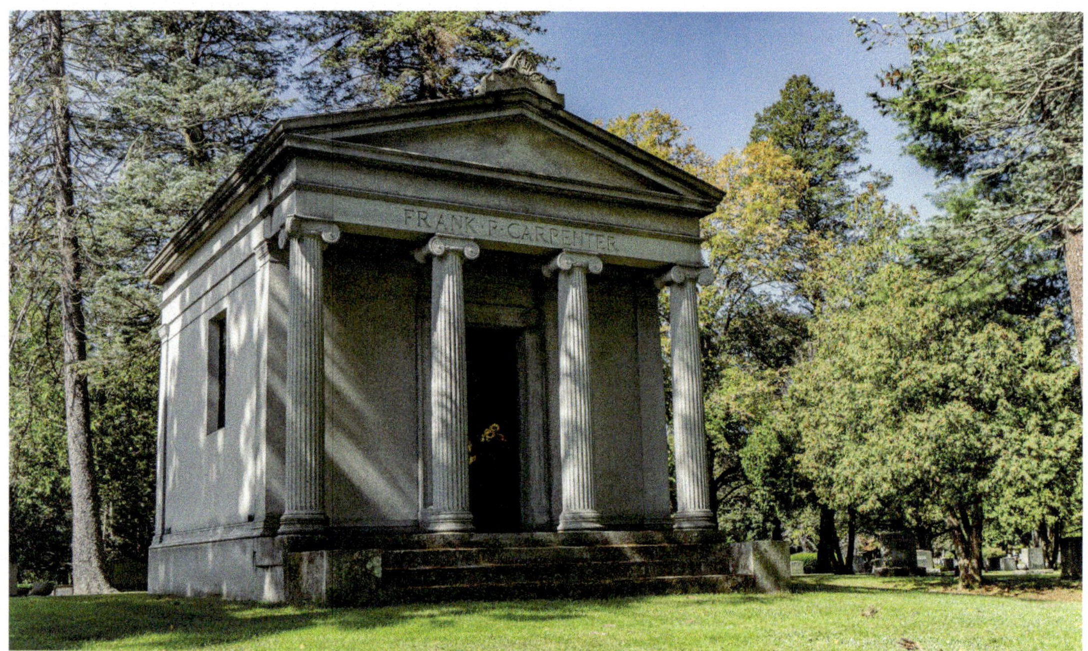

Frank Carpenter, entrepreneur.

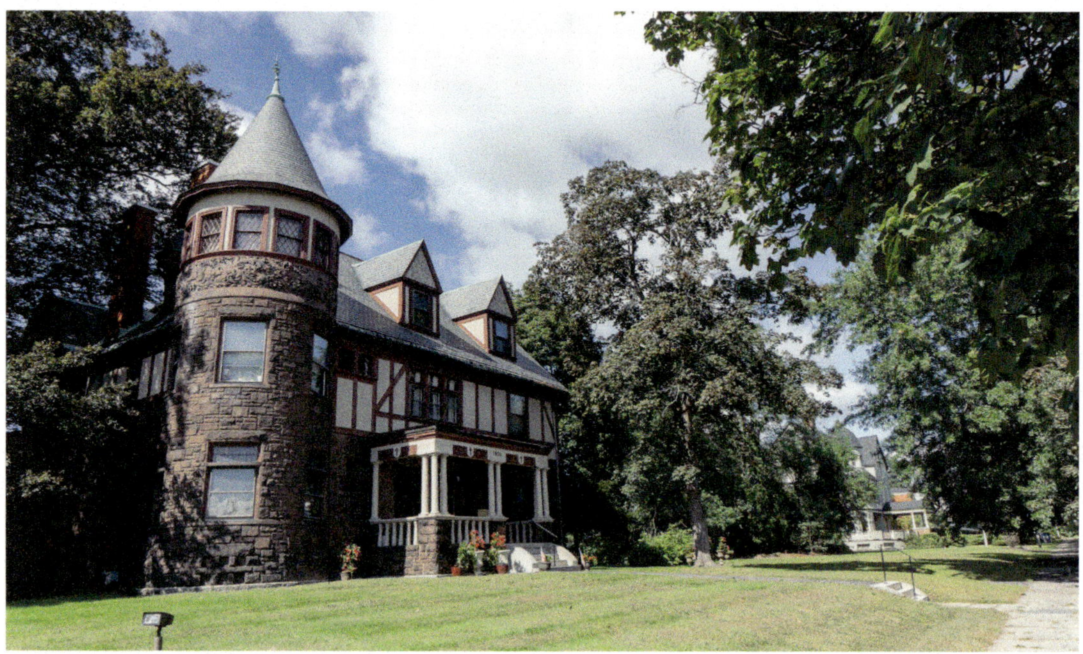

Frank Carpenter's home.

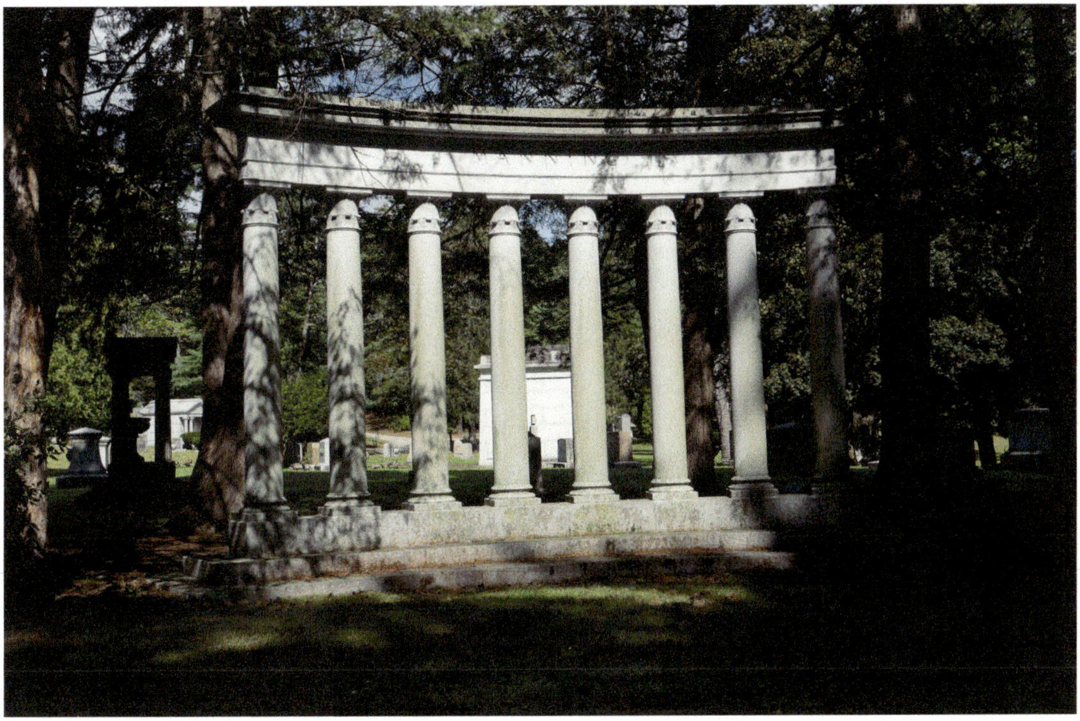

Manning family.

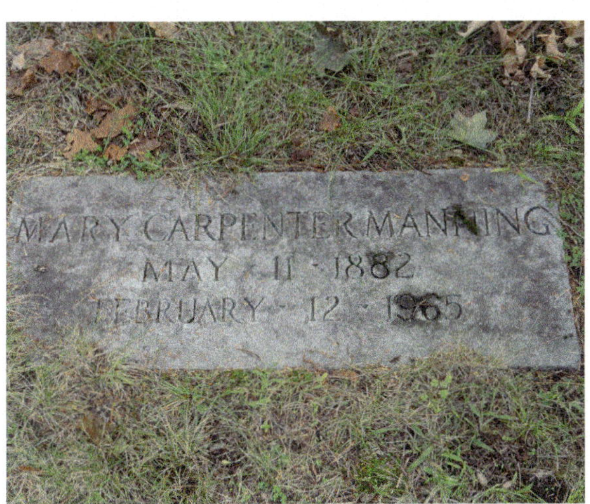

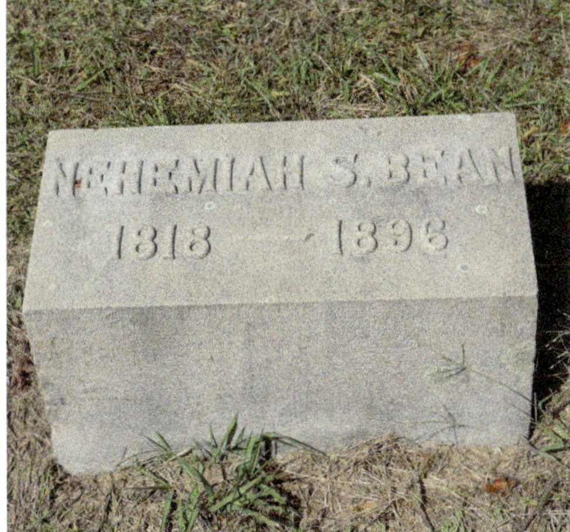

Above left: Mary Carpenter Manning, Frank Carpenter's daughter.

Above right: Nehemiah S. Bean, steam fire engine inventor.

The Old Burying Ground or The Old Dunstable Burying Ground, Nashua

This small historical cemetery is set beside the Daniel Webster Highway, at one of the busiest intersections in the state. A little bit of solace in a sea of twenty-first-century chaos is flanked by a Walgreens superstore and a huge mall across the highway. It is doubtful that many of the motorists waiting out the traffic lights even notice the old cemetery, much less know anything about the history of those interned there.

The cemetery was once the site of the Second Meeting House of Dunstable, Massachusetts. The border between Massachusetts and New Hampshire was changed in 1741 by Royal Decree. Today, the Old Burial Ground is part of Nashua. Rev. Thomas Weld is buried here; he was ordained at the Second Meeting House in 1685 and served as the first minister until his death in 1704. A memorial marker states that he died defending his flock during an Indian raid. This appears untrue and is stated in the Nashua Town History. However, Thomas Lund's grave is inscribed: "Memento Mori. Here lies the body of Mr. Thomas Lund, who departed this life on Sept. 5, 1724, in the 42nd-year of his age. This man with seven more that lies in this grave was slew all in a day by the Indians." The actual number may be as high as fifteen. Several veterans of the Battle of Bunker Hill are buried here, including Col. Bancroft, whose stone is inscribed: "In Memory of Col. Ebenezer Bancroft, who died Sept. 22, 1827. Act. 90. He was an officer in the French War, the American Revolution, and the Battle of Bunker Hill." A captain at the time, he fought valiantly and was wounded. It is said that he was the last man off the hill. He wrote an excellent account of the battle that survives today.

Visitors to the cemetery will notice the lovely, brick one-room schoolhouse built in 1841. The school was restored in 1976 and is visited annually by Nashua's fourth graders as part of their history curriculum. They spend a day at the old school dressed in period clothing, learning what attending school in the nineteenth century was like.

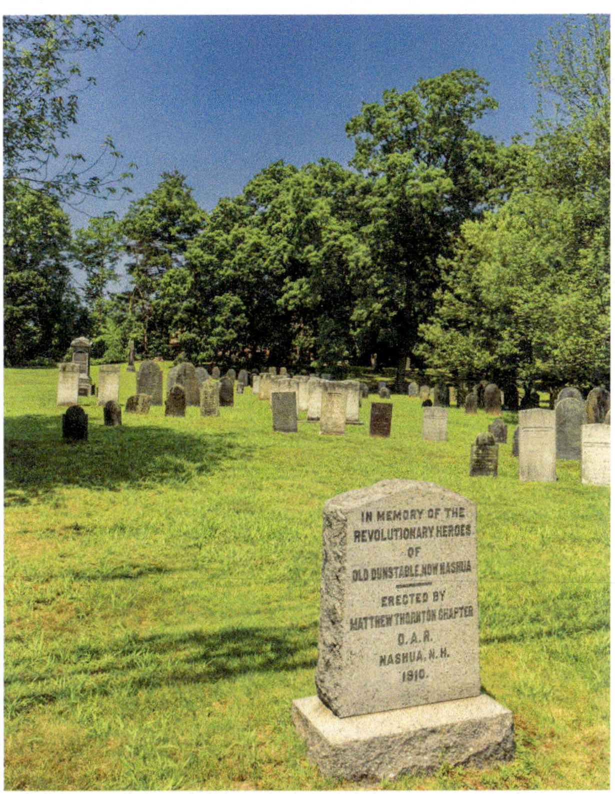

Old Burial Ground, Nashua.

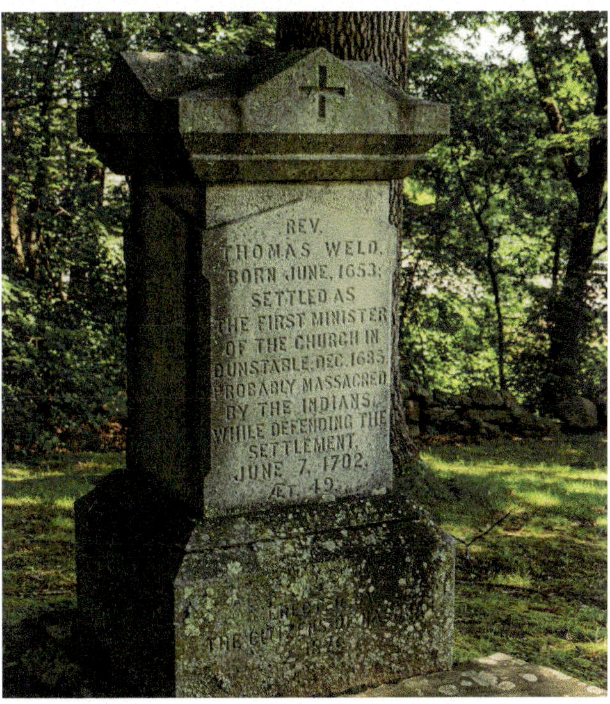

Grave of Reverend Thomas Weld,
Nashua.

2
HISTORICAL FIGURES

Josiah Bartlett (1729–1795), Plains Cemetery, Kingston

Josiah Bartlett is best known for being the second signer of the American Declaration of Independence after John Hancock. Martin Sheen's portrayal of President Jed Bartlett, a fictional direct descendent of Dr. Josiah Bartlett in the TV series *West Wing*, further increased his reputation as a founding father. Josiah's political career began as a member of the New Hampshire British Colony's Provincial Assembly. Before revolutionary sympathizers forced Tory Governor John Wentworth to leave New Hampshire, he stripped Bartlett of his official colonial duties. The Bartlett's homestead burned. It was allegedly set on fire by the Tories because of Bartlett's sympathies with the revolutionaries. Initially, Bartlett declined an appointment with John Pickering to the Continental Congress so that he could attend to his family and home. He accepted later as the only delegate until he, through repeated requests, convinced the New Hampshire Assembly to additionally send William Whipple and Matthew Thornton. In 1777, he did not return to Philadelphia but served as a physician with John Stark at the Battle of Bennington. He later rejoined the Continental Congress, where he helped write, argue for, and cast the first vote for the proposed Articles of Confederation.

After this, he was drawn back to New Hampshire to serve his home state as a delegate to the New Hampshire Convention to adopt the United States Constitution. He also served as a judge on the New Hampshire Supreme Court and as president of the state. The title of president was changed to governor during Bartlett's term. He also was the first president of the New Hampshire Medical Society. During his own time, he was known as a physician. He began studying medicine when he was sixteen years old and set up his medical practice in Kingston when he was twenty-one. By all accounts, he didn't shy away from trying new remedies often on himself. He cured himself of a life-threatening fever by drinking cold cider. He stressed the importance of not drinking hot liquids to cure fever and rejected covering patients with heavy blankets in a hot room. He was among the first physicians to use quinine extracted from Peruvian bark to treat diphtheria. Dr. Josiah Bartlett's reputed, unquenchable thirst for knowledge served him well as a doctor and a man who effectively served his country and the State of New Hampshire.

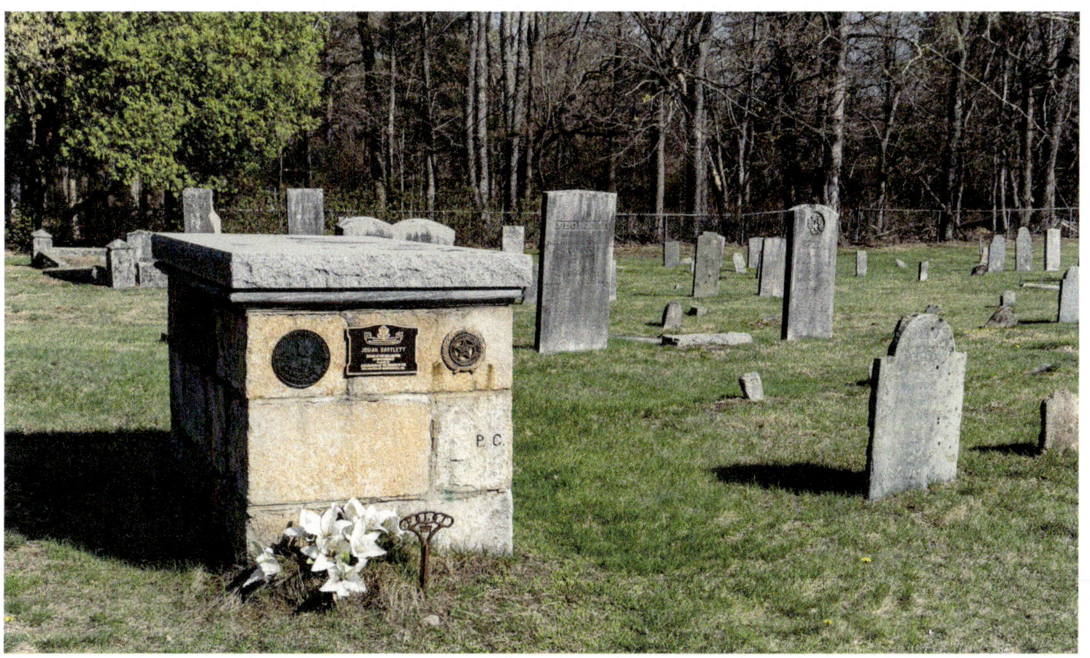

Grave of Josiah Bartlett.

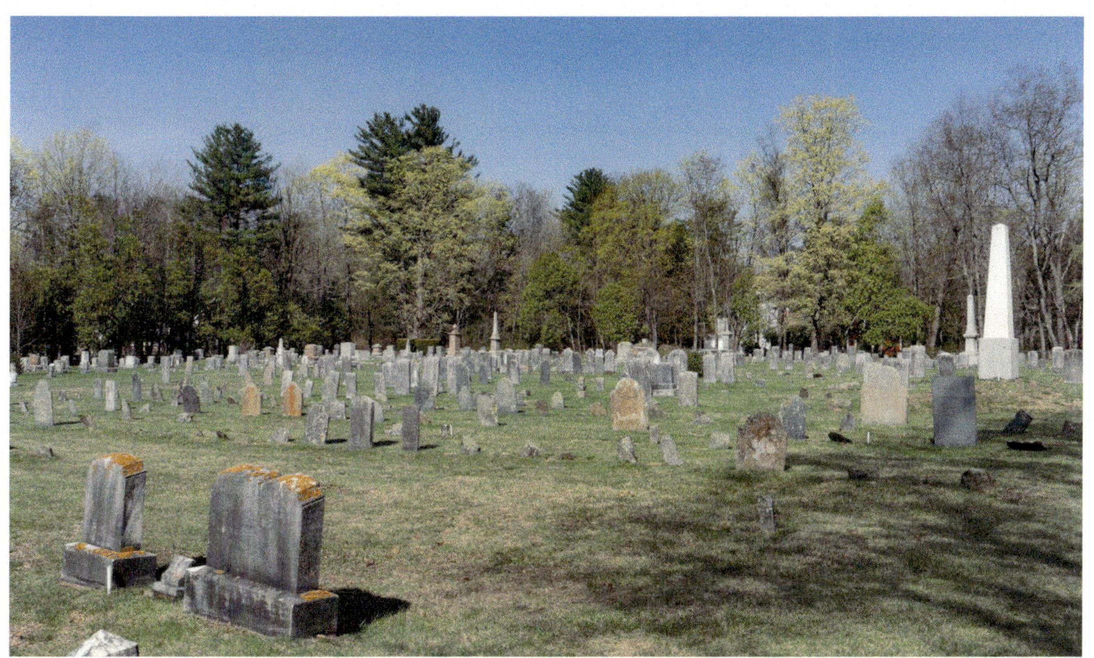

Plains Cemetery, Kingston.

Alan Shepard (1923–1998), Forest Hills Cemetery, East Derry

Alan Bartlett Shepard Jr. went from a one-room schoolhouse in Derry, New Hampshire, to become the second person and the first American in space. In 1971, he landed on the moon along with Edgar Mitchell. Stuart Roosa operated the space capsule. His first trip as an astronaut was in 1961. His Mercury spacecraft took him 116 miles into the sky. The second, Apollo 14, landed on the moon, giving Shepard and Mitchell enough time to walk, collect over 100 pounds of moon rocks, and conduct experiments. Shepard hit three golf balls. The last one went for 200 yards. Shepard claimed he got the idea from Bob Hope. The comedian always carried a golf club. It was a decent experiment to see how far the ball would go in low gravity. At forty-seven, Shepard was the fifth and oldest person to walk on the moon. Both Bill and I were fourteen when Alan Shepard took his first flight. I remember watching that event on black and white television at Kennett Junior High School in Conway. It was a very thrilling fifteen minutes and thirty seconds. Teachers and students cheered when it was clear that the mission had been successful. The Russians had put Yuri Gagarin into space twenty-three days before Shepard made his trip. Ground control operated Gagarin's capsule, but Shepard was the first astronaut to navigate his spacecraft manually.

Shepard's one-room schoolhouse led to Pinkerton Academy, the Naval Academy, service on a ship during World War II, later the rank of rear admiral, and to too many awards and recognitions to list here. After the war, he trained as a test pilot and participated in NASA's first astronaut class. At one point, he was almost dropped from Naval Flight School. He took private flying lessons to develop his skills to pass the Navy's test. Shepard also suffered from an inner ear disease that caused dizziness and nausea. This illness prevented him from joining the Gemini Mission and might have meant the end of his flying career. Surgery corrected this condition before the Apollo 14 mission. He had a reputation for being demanding and was referred to by some as the "icy commander."

On the other hand, he could be the life of the party. He and his wife, Louise Brewer Shepard, spent over fifty years together with their two daughters and a niece, whom they raised. Astronauts and their wives are indeed heroic figures. One can only imagine the stress on the families and the astronauts themselves. Alan and Louise died within five weeks of each other. Their ashes were scattered together near their home in California. Their cenotaphs are in the Forest Hill Cemetery in East Derry. You could check out Tom Wolfe's *The Right Stuff*. There is also a film and a TV series under the same name. Note that Shepard was not a fan of Wolfe's book. His book, written with fellow astronaut Deke Slayton, was titled *Moon Shot*, which Shepard called the "real stuff."

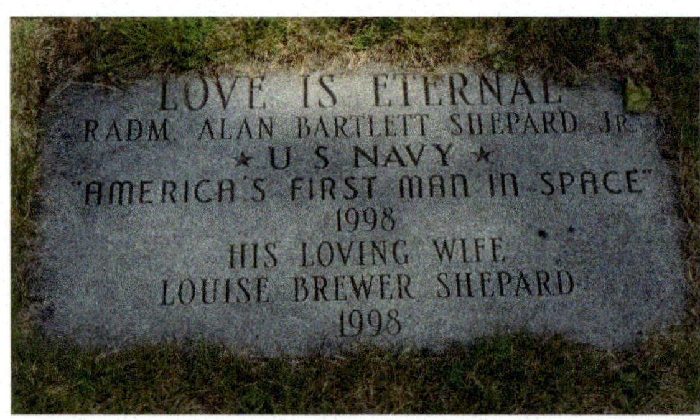

Cenotaph of Alan Shepard.

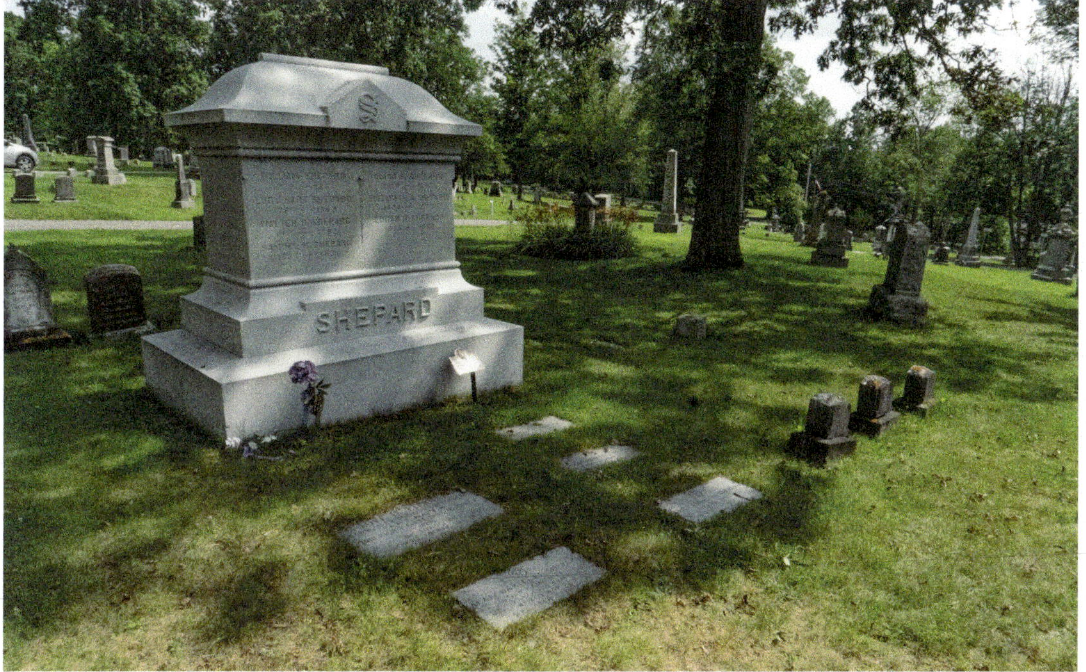

Shepard family.

Matthew Thornton (1714–1803), Thornton Cemetery, Merrimack

Matthew Thornton was one of three signers of the American Declaration of Independence from New Hampshire. He, Josiah Bartlett, and William Whipple played prominent roles in New Hampshire's history. Matthew's parents emigrated to America from Ireland around 1717 and settled in either Wiscasset or Brunswick in what would become Maine. When Matthew was eight years old, he and his family escaped by canoe from their burning home after an attack by native tribes. One way or another, they went to Worcester, Massachusetts, where Matthew grew up and went to school. He studied medicine in Leicester, Massachusetts, and established his medical practice in Londonderry, New Hampshire. In 1745, Thornton served as a surgeon for the New Hampshire Militia during the Crown's successful expedition to attack Fortress Louisbourg in Nova Scotia. Despite his opposition to the Stamp Act, he was commissioned as a colonel in the British Militia under Benning Wentworth. He also served as royal justice of the peace and in the New Hampshire Provincial Assembly. Once the French were no longer a threat after the French and Indian War, many once loyal British subjects began to question the increased taxation and regulations coming from the British Parliament, Prime Minister Lord North, and King George III. Dr. Thornton joined the civilian resistance to taxation without representation and tyrannical abuse of power. He was elected president of the New Hampshire Provincial Assembly, served on the New Hampshire Committee of Safety, and helped draft the first New Hampshire Constitution.

New Hampshire was the first of the original colonies to adopt such a government plan. This constitution delegated executive power to a committee of safety, which functioned when the legislature was not in session.

He was elected to the Continental Congress after the "Declaration of Independence" was officially signed in August 1776. Although he arrived in Philadelphia in November of that year, he was allowed to add his signature to the "Declaration of Independence." He was not a lawyer, but he was made an associate judge of the New Hampshire Supreme Court. He also served as a Londonderry selectman, state senate member, and New Hampshire counselor. Later in life, he retired from medicine, became a political essayist, and farmed and operated Thornton's Ferry with his wife and family. The town of Thornton is named after him. The State of New Hampshire erected a memorial to Matthew Thornton, recognizing him as a signer of the Declaration of Independence in the Thornton Cemetery across the street from the home he built for his son James. James ran the home as a tavern but eventually committed suicide in that house. Today, the building houses a Common Man Restaurant and is reputed to be haunted. Matthew's grave sits among family members, including James, in the Thornton Cemetery, and although obscured with age, reads: "The Honest Man." Bill and I wondered why the other New Hampshire signers of the Declaration have not had stately monuments erected in their memory. I stumbled across a reference to a letter from Meshech Weare, chairman of the committee of safety of New Hampshire, to Thornton and William Whipple, pointing out that the troops' wages were insufficient to support them. You can't help but wonder about the interpersonal relationships of all these supporters of the American Revolution.

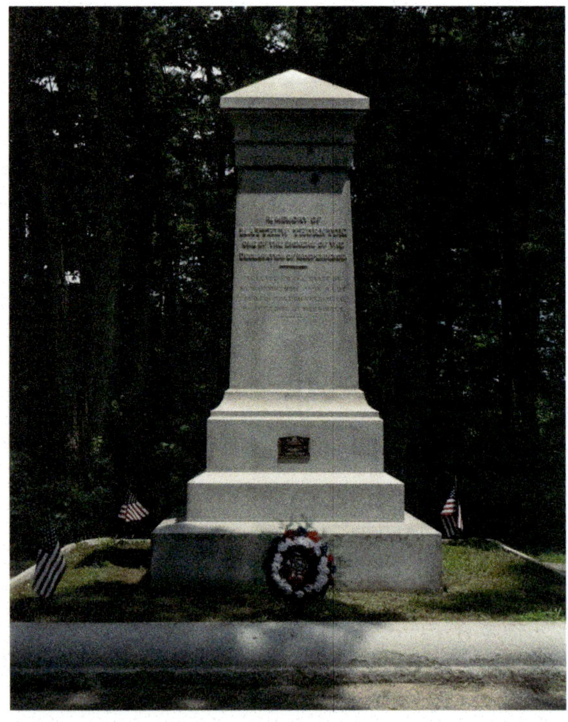

Matthew Thornton monument.

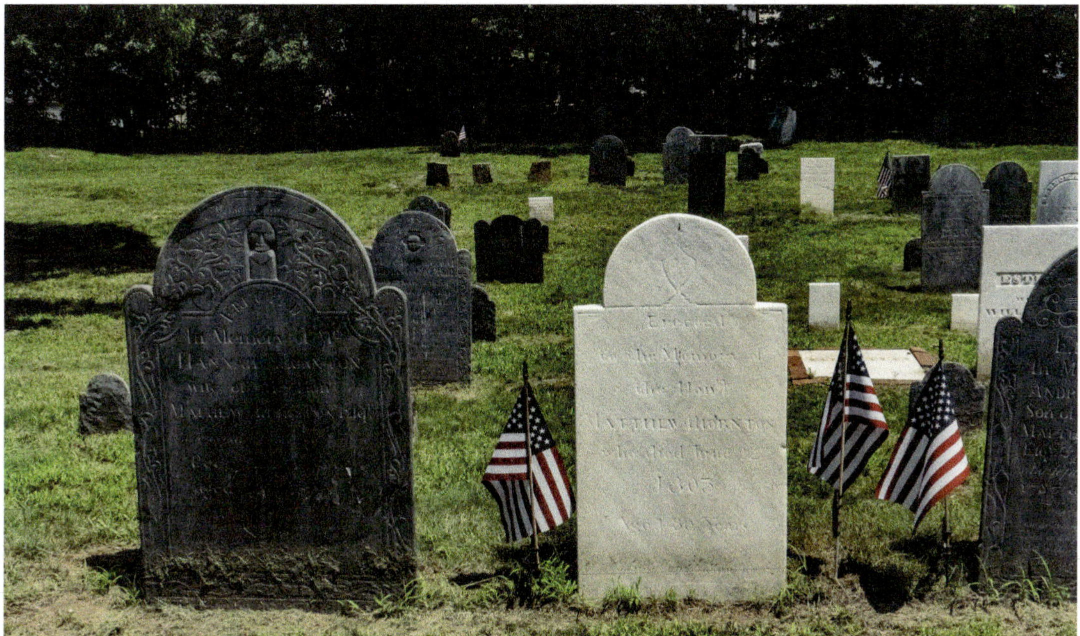

Grave of Matthew Thornton.

James S. Thornton (1826–1875), Civil War Naval Hero, Last Rest Cemetery, Merrimac

Born in Merrimack in 1826, James S. Thornton was a direct descendant of Matthew Thornton, one of three signers of the Declaration of Independence from New Hampshire. He entered the U.S. Navy in 1841 as a midshipman and served during the Mexican War. In the Civil War, he was the executive officer of the *Hartford*, Farragut's flagship. He was present at the capture of New Orleans. As commander of the gunship *Winona* at Mobile Bay, he successfully destroyed a Confederate steamer. Later assigned as the executive officer aboard the sloop of war USS *Kearsarge*, Thornton saw his greatest action against the blockade runner *Alabama*.

The *Alabama* was the pride of the Confederacy and had wreaked havoc with Union merchant ships. Under the command of Captain Raphael Semmes, the *Alabama* had taken refuge in the French port of Cherbourg, where she had gone for repairs and coaling. France was a neutral nation and had given Semmes the choice of taking on coal or repairs and to make quick. The *Kearsarge* arrived at the mouth of the port, trapping the *Alabama*. Semmes's only options were to stay in port and let his ship go to rot or come out fighting. He chose to fight.

The die was cast, and the two ships, quite evenly matched, would be pitted against each other in a do-or-die battle—much to the delight of the French, who turned out to watch the duel in droves. Special trains brought spectators from all over the country. As it turned out, they had a good show. At 9:45 a.m., on June 18, the *Alabama* steamed out of Cherbourg to meet the *Kearsarge*. Both crews and ships gave a good account of themselves. However, the *Alabama* was defeated and sank. Captain Winslow and his EO, Thornton, would be honored by Congress for their victory and courage.

On a side note, the USS *Kearsarge* was named for Mount Kearsarge. The problem is that there are two mountains in New Hampshire named Kearsarge; one is in North Conway, and the other is in Warner. Both towns claim the ship was named after their mountain, which has been hotly disputed over the years. In truth, both sides have some valid arguments. Capt. Winslow is buried in Forest Hill Cemetery in Boston. His marker is a boulder from the mountain in Warner.

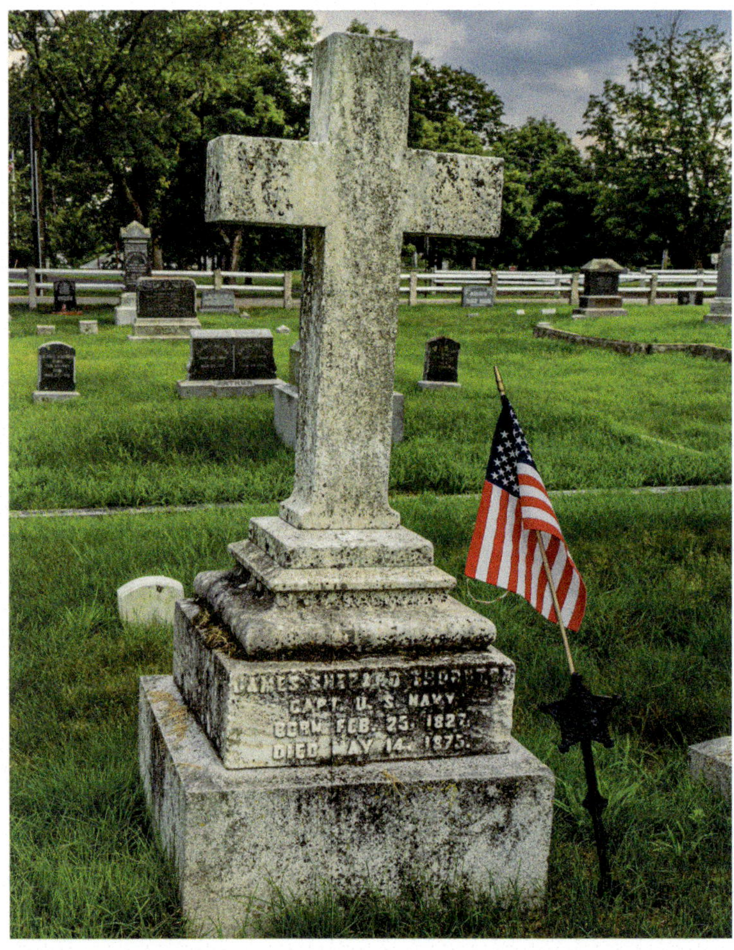

Captain James Thornton.

Virgil White, Riverside Cemetery, Tamworth

The Ford Model T, often called the Flivver, was quite versatile. Jack up the rear and remove one tire, add a drive belt, and you have a power plant for perhaps milling grain, powering a lumber mill, or propelling a rope tow for skiing. One drawback to the Flivver was that it didn't drive well in the snow when winter rolled around. You had to resort to horse and sleigh for half the year while your Ford sat on blocks. Virgil D. White was the authorized Ford dealer in West Ossipee who sold and maintained Ford Vehicles at White's Garage. He was also an inventor. In 1913, White patented the plans for a conversion kit for the Model T. This kit featured skis for the front of the vehicle and two extra heavy-duty wheels for the rear that could accept caterpillar-style tracks. He also developed tracks for other environments, such as sandy soil. He copyrighted the name Snowmobile.

White marketed the final version in 1922. You could then purchase a modified Model T that could travel up to 18 miles per hour in deep snow. Henry Ford authorized the sale of conversion kits for $400, and you could buy a fully converted model for $750. Doctors, delivery truck drivers, milkmen, mail carriers, fire departments, and anyone who needed to get around in the snow became customers. A Model T Snowmobile was part of Calvin Coolidge's funeral procession. So, it seems Ossipee can claim to be the home of the first Snowmobile. White sold seventy of his modified vehicles in 1923 and 1924. He eventually sold the rights to the Farm Specialty Manufacturing Company; they produced 3,300 a year until 1929, when the factory burned. The company went out of business. Other entrepreneurs would build on the concept to create the Snowmobile as we know it today. A memorial in the Riverside Cemetery in Tamworth commemorates Virgil D. White as a highly regarded commissioner of motor vehicles in New Hampshire.

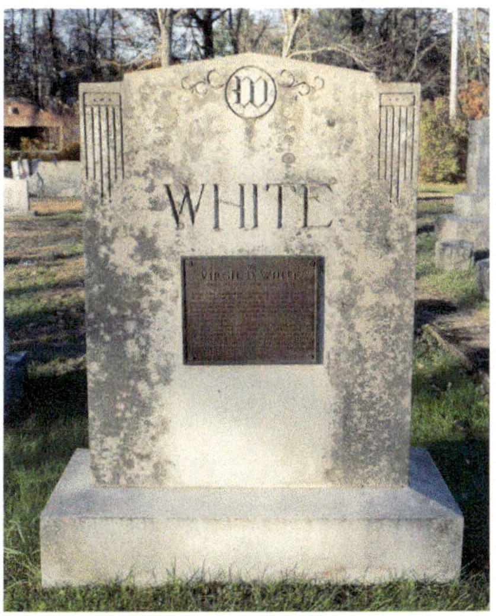

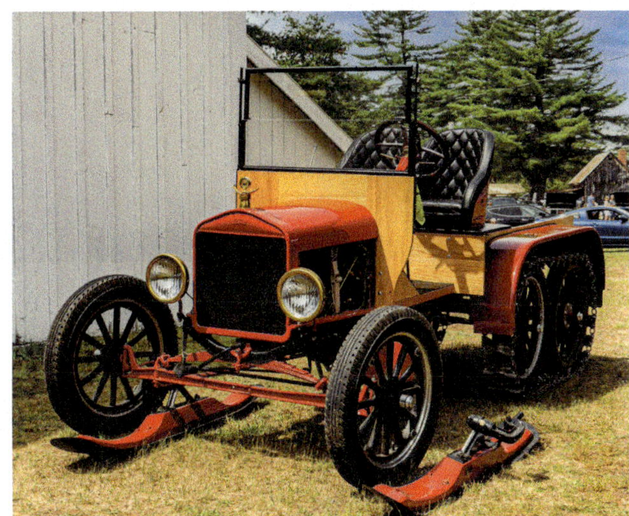

Above left: Grave of Virgil White.

Above right: Virgil White's Model T snowmobile conversion.

Hannah Davis (1784–1863), Old Burial Ground, Jaffrey

Hannah Davis was a self-made woman and entrepreneur. Having lost both her parents and grandparents, her success was born out of necessity. Born in 1784, her father was a clockmaker, and her grandfather a millwright, which undoubtedly contributed to her craft skills. When her mother died, she was forced to fend for herself. She began by constructing band boxes in her shed. A bandbox is more commonly known as a hat box, although they were used to store other items such as shoes and clothing. Band boxes were common at the time; they were made from pasteboard and covered in wallpaper. Hannah made her boxes from thin slices of spruce fastened with nails. The boxes were lined with local newspapers (which help date existing boxes) and covered in brightly colored wallpaper. She invented her own machine to slice the spruce to the correct thickness of 1/16 of an inch. At first, she marketed her boxes locally but soon branched out by transporting them to Manchester and Lowell. They were very popular with mill girls, and she often parked her wagon in front of a mill and sold directly to the girls. Boxes retailed from 12 to 50 cents. Today, her boxes are highly collectible and can fetch over $1,000. Hannah marked the inside of her boxes with a label that read: "Warranted-Nailed, Band Boxes, Hand Made by Hannah Davis, Jaffrey, NH." She was most active between 1820 and 1855. When she broke her hip, she retired to a small home that still stands on Main Street in Jaffrey today. Known as "Aunt Hannah," she was well-liked by her neighbors, who contributed to her care until her death in 1863. She is buried in the Old Burial Ground in Jaffrey.

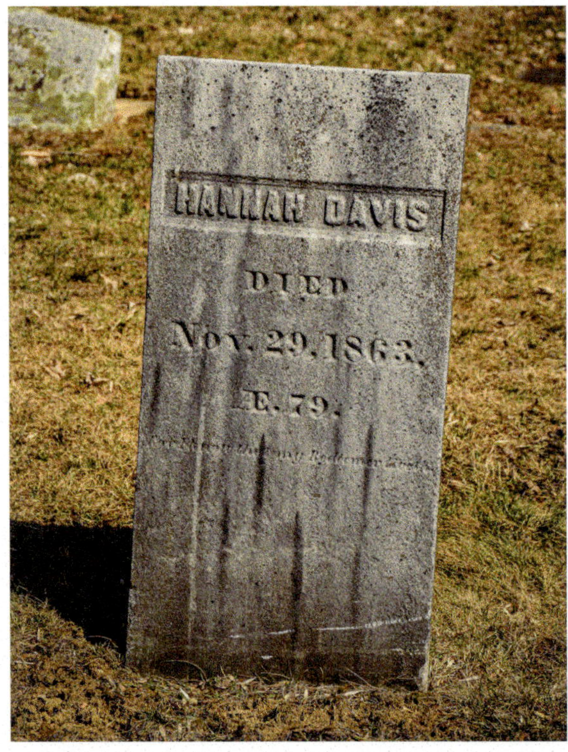

Grave of Hannah Davis.

Reverend Robert Jordan (1611–1679), New Castle

Reverend Robert Jordan was an influential figure among the early settlers of Maine and New Hampshire. Among other places, Jordan served as pastor of the Isle of Shoals and New Castle. His house still stands in New Castle, and he was buried nearby in 1679. He was a respected Anglican Minister, apparently successful in business and known as a skilled negotiator. This is from the family records of the Jordan Family: "…the fact that, at the conclusion of a long life, he left to numerous heirs a large and very valuable estate, sufficiently exhibit him as a man of no ordinary powers." One of those distant heirs, Bruce Jordan, is a good friend and classmate from Bowdoin College. So, Bill and I decided that Reverend Jordan deserved to be included in our book. We set out to find the memorial in New Castle that marked the Reverend's final resting place. It was a beautiful winter day, and we enjoyed the search, but it was fruitless. We talked to several residents who knew nothing of the memorial. We even called Bruce and continued looking based on his recollections of visiting the site. This was to no avail. We learned from one of our conversations with a local that the Reverend Jordan's classic colonial home had been purchased and renovated. There had been, apparently, local efforts to save the house from that fate. Ironically, a local man told us it sits near, but is not included in, an area in New Castle set aside to protect historically significant buildings. The renovations are, I guess, impressive, but something has been lost. It's a burial site we couldn't find. Apparently, the marker had been removed.

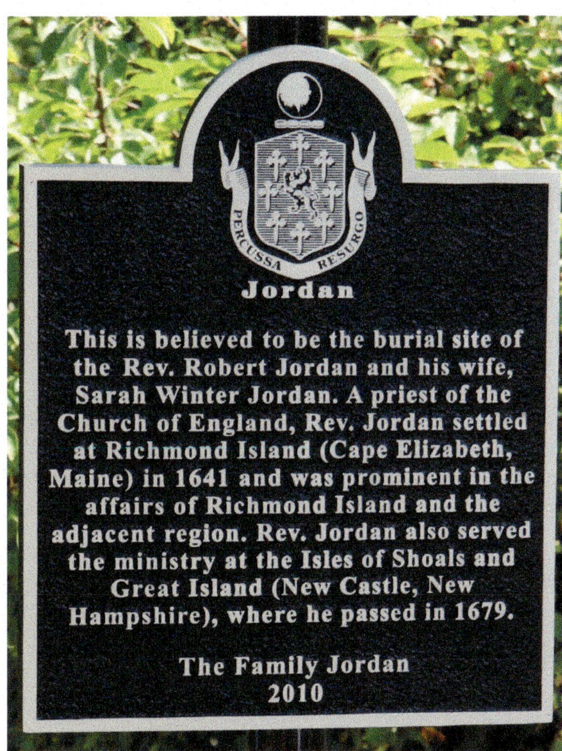

Reverend Robert Jordan historical marker.

Benning Wentworth (1696–1770), New Hampshire's First Colonial Governor, St. John's Church, Portsmouth

The impressive St. John's Episcopal Church sits in the heart of Portsmouth's Strawberry Bank. The Episcopal congregation of Portsmouth dates to 1832. The first church, a wood structure, was constructed in 1732 and destroyed in a devastating fire that consumed over 300 buildings in the city. The present-day church, the first brick church in New Hampshire, was built on the same site in 1807.

The cemetery dates to the original church and is the final resting place of some of Portsmouth's earliest influential residents. Most well-known are those of the Wentworth family, including the first colonial Governor of New Hampshire, Benning Wentworth. The Wentworth family were well-to-do merchants who imported wine from Spain. New Hampshire was part of the Massachusetts Colony, but the Wentworth family favored separation from Massachusetts. They were only successful once Benning Wentworth was elected to the Massachusetts Assembly and two years later was on the Governor's Council. He was not popular with his peers due to his support of separating; however, in 1744, New Hampshire gained its independence from Massachusetts, and Benning became the first governor. From the very first, Wentworth set out to expand the colony and his wealth. He did so by granting townships to the north and west to present-day Vermont, then part of New York. Bennington, Vermont, is named after him. He became wealthy and was known to flaunt his wealth by parading about Portsmouth in a luxurious carriage. Despite this, he was well-liked by the people of New Hampshire. Castle Freeman Jr. wrote in an article for *Harvard Magazine*:

> For all his luxury and hauteur, however, the common people of New Hampshire seem to have loved him. They smiled when, at 64, the widowed Wentworth scandalized polite Portsmouth by marrying his housekeeper, a woman young enough to be his granddaughter; and when he died at Little Harbor ten years later, they mourned.

One of his biographers has speculated that our history might have turned out very differently if the crown had appointed more governors with Wentworth's abilities. Wentworth retired not long before colonial unrest led to the American Revolution.

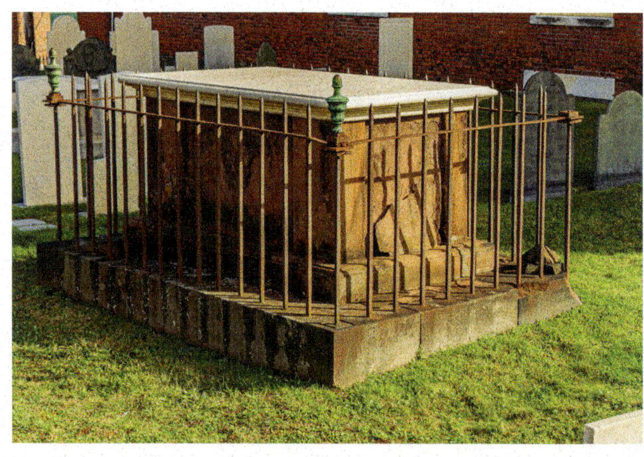

Wentworth family tomb, Saint Johns' Church.

Louis Downing (1792–1873), Old North Cemetery, Concord

John Ford and John Wayne would never have made the movie *Stagecoach* without Louis Downing of Concord, New Hampshire. Downing was the maker of the famous Concord Coach. If Winchester and Colt provided the firearms that won the West, Downing and his partner J. Stephen Abbot provided the transportation. Louis Downing was a wheelwright from Lexington, Massachusetts, who married a girl from Concord. While visiting his soon-to-be wife, he decided Concord might be an excellent place to start a business. In 1813, he set up a carriage shop on the north end of town. It took him a year to build his first wagon by himself. Three years later, he purchased property in the city's south end and employed several workers. Downing hired Abbot in 1826 to build coach bodies. Soon after, the company became Abbot and Downing.

Downing invented a system where the coach's body, instead of being mounted directly to the axles, was suspended on leather straps and hung on posts supported by the axle. The result was a much more comfortable ride for the passengers, and it was easier for the coach to traverse rough terrain. In his book *Roughing It*, Mark Twain spoke of the Concord Coach: "Our coach was a great swinging and swaying stage, of the most sumptuous description—an imposing cradle on wheels."

The Concord Coach was the Rolls-Royce of its day, made to exact standards of the highest quality. Ben Holladay, the owner of the Overland Stage Company, ordered 110 Concord Coaches, and when he sold out to Wells Fargo, they purchased an additional thirty. Ultimately, the company was a victim of the railroads, and in 1909, it declared bankruptcy. The company tried to make truck bodies for a short while, but soon, that also failed. The last Concord Coach was made in 1915.

Downing made a considerable contribution to winning the West without ever leaving Concord.

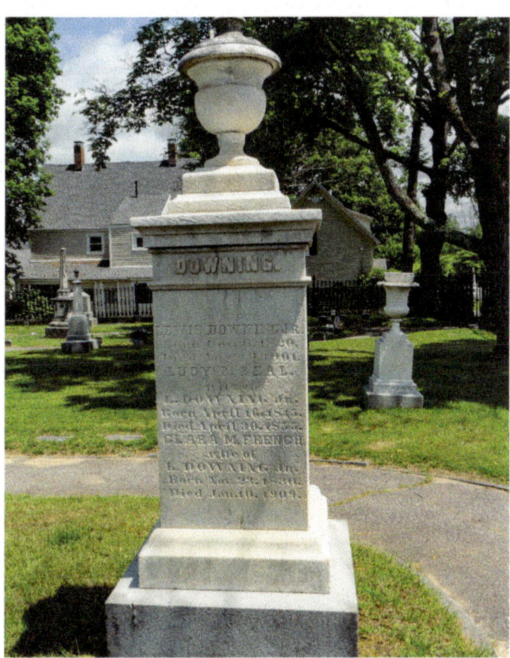

Grave of Louis Downing.

Wentworth Cheswill, First Black American to Hold Public Office in America, New Market

In December 1774, two riders were dispatched from Boston to Portsmouth. New Hampshire. The two riders were Paul Revere and Wentworth Cheswill. The message they carried warned that two British warships were on their way to reinforce Fort William and Mary in New Castle. The next day, 400 patriots captured the fort and removed the arms and powder. The ships never got to New Castle and the captured munitions were later used in the Siege of Boston.

Wentworth Cheswill, sometimes spelled Cheswell, was the grandson of an African American slave. He is listed in the Newmarket census as white, although he was probably considered a "mulatto." Wentworth served as a soldier in the War for Independence and fought at Saratoga. He is credited as being the first African American to hold public office in America and New Hampshire's first archeologist. He had received his education at Governor Dummer Academy and served as a schoolmaster in Newmarket. His first elected office was that of town constable in 1768. He went on to hold several offices in the town, including selectman, assessor, and justice of the peace. He was a man of science and collected Native American artifacts around Newmarket.

Wentworth is buried in the family cemetery in Newmarket with his wife, Mary Davis Cheswill, and six children. In 2007, a New Hampshire historical marker was placed in front of the cemetery.

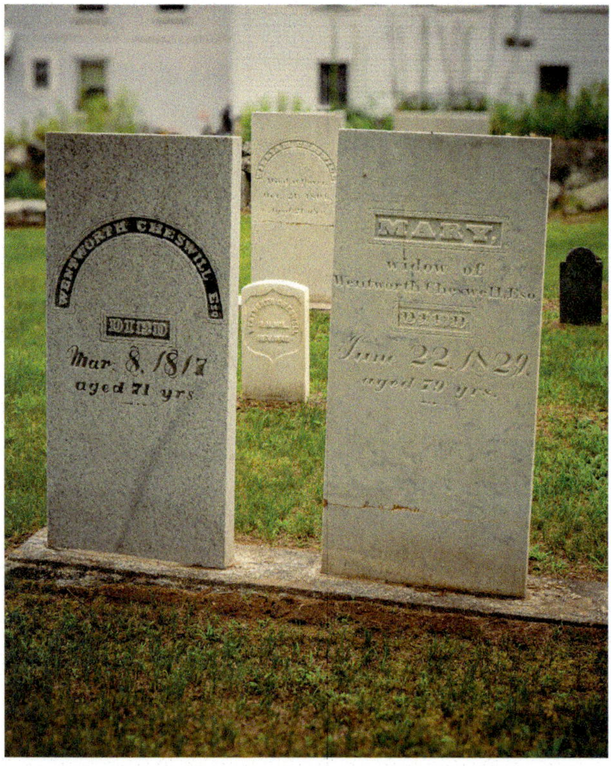

Wentworth Cheswell family cemetery.

Amos Fortune (died 1801), The Old Burying Ground, Jaffery

One of New Hampshire's most historic and prettiest cemeteries is the Old Burying Ground in Jaffrey. To say that it is picturesque would be an understatement. It sits behind the town's original meetinghouse with a spectacular view of Mount Monadnock. The meetinghouse is classic New England. It was raised in June 1775, the same day that the Battle of Bunker Hill was being fought. The Burial Ground has a fair share of New Hampshire notables. Among them is Amos Fortune.

Amos Fortune was a hardworking, God-fairing man who gave back to his community and would probably have been forgotten as just another citizen of Jaffrey had he not been born a slave. His tombstone inscription reads: "Sacred to the memory of Amos Fortune, who was born free in Africa, a slave in America, he purchased Liberty, professed Christianity, lived reputably, and died hopefully November 17, 1801, AEt. 91."

As a slave to Ichabod Richardson of Woburn, Massachusetts, he had an arrangement to purchase his freedom; however, Richardson died, and the matter was unsettled. Fortune was able to renegotiate with his former master's heirs and became a freeman in 1770 at the age of sixty. Fortune continued to live and work in Woburn. He purchased his first wife, Lydia Somerset, in 1775 from Josiah Bowers of Billerica. Sadly, she died within the year. Fortune purchased a second wife, Violate or Violet, from James Baldwin on November 9, 1779, and married her on the same day in Woburn. They would later adopt a daughter named Celyndia. While in Woburn, he purchased land and built a home with the help of his former mistress. In 1781, he moved to Jaffrey, New Hampshire.

In Jaffrey, Violate and Amos made a good life for themselves. Amos owned his own tanning business and had at least two apprentices. He was able to purchase 25 acres of land upon which he built a home—still standing today on Amos Fortune Road. A philanthropist both during his life and after. Amos was a contributor to the Jaffrey Social Library, and in his will, after provisions were made for his wife and daughter, he left money to the church and the local school. The Amos Fortune Fund was later created for his adopted town to support public speaking contests and special publications. The fund continues today and is administered by the Jaffrey Public Library. Various well-known speakers are invited to speak each year at the historic meetinghouse. The legacy stands as a remarkable achievement for a man who was bound in slavery for two-thirds of his ninety-one years.

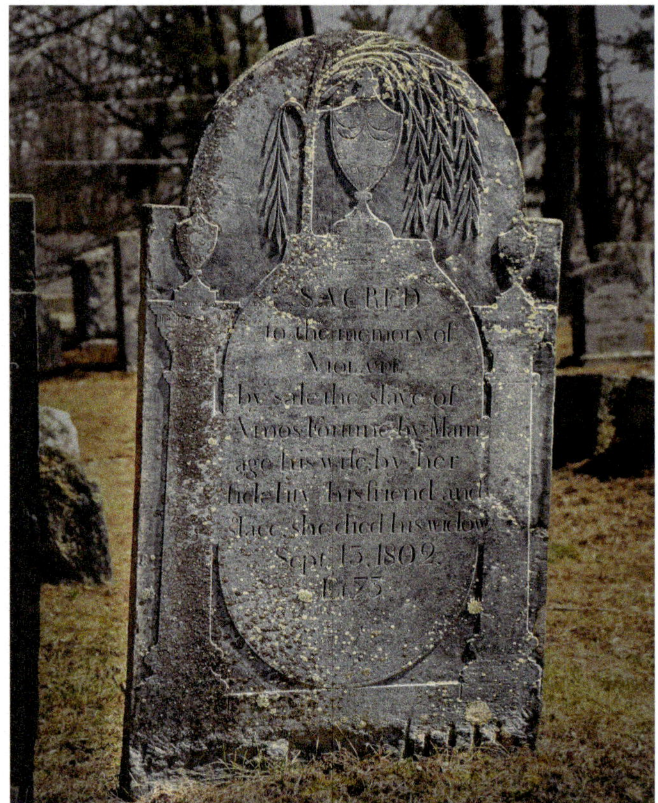

Amos Fortune.

Lucy Lambert Hale (1841–1915), Pine Hill Cemetery, Dover

Lucy Lambert Hale was attractive and quite a sensation in her time. Her admirers included Oliver Wendell Holmes Jr., Robert Todd Lincoln, Lincoln's private secretary John Hay, and titled aristocrats. She is most famous for her relationship with John Wilkes Booth, and she was apparently secretly engaged to Wilkes Booth at the time that he assassinated President Abraham Lincoln at Ford's Theater. When Wilkes Booth was captured and shot, authorities found pictures of five women along with his diary. One of those pictures was of Lucy Hale. How did a passionate supporter of the South and slavery and the daughter of John Parker Hale, a former senator, presidential candidate, and well-known vocal abolitionist, fall in love with each other? Lucy was a star in Washington, D.C., society. John Wilkes Booth was a celebrity from a famous theatrical family and was well known as an actor and heartthrob, much like some performers today. He was also an infamous playboy. He introduced himself to Lucy by sending her an anonymous Valentine's Day letter. By 1865, the couple was seen together in public, and John even attended Lincoln's second inauguration with a ticket Lucy obtained for him from her father. A photograph shows him there with fellow conspirators.

There is no evidence that Lucy knew about her fiancé's plan to kidnap the president, but she must have known about his ardent support of the Confederacy. On the day of the assassination, Lucy apparently spent time studying Spanish with Robert Todd Lincoln and John Hay. Witnesses said Lucy and Booth had been together at the National Hotel that morning. They were staying in the hotel and had dinner with Lucy's mother before Wilkes Booth, after quoting Shakespeare, went to Ford's theater to become one of the most infamous assassins in United States history. Lucy expressed grief and disbelief that her fiancé could have committed such a horrendous act. Legend has it that a veiled mourning woman visited a tugboat carrying Booth's body, but there is no evidence that this was Lucy Hale. Lucy wasn't the only woman grieving Booth's death. In any case, Lucy went to Spain with her family, where her father served as ambassador. No one in the Hale family was asked to testify after the assassination, and Lucy eventually married William E. Chandler, a former suitor and widower. Chandler was a lawyer, U.S. senator, newspaper publisher, and secretary of the navy. A naval destroyer was named after him. Lucy supported her husband in his endeavors and was a devoted and civic-minded wife. She and her husband raised money to erect a monument to her father in front of the New Hampshire State House. The Hale family home is part of the Woodman Museum in Dover.

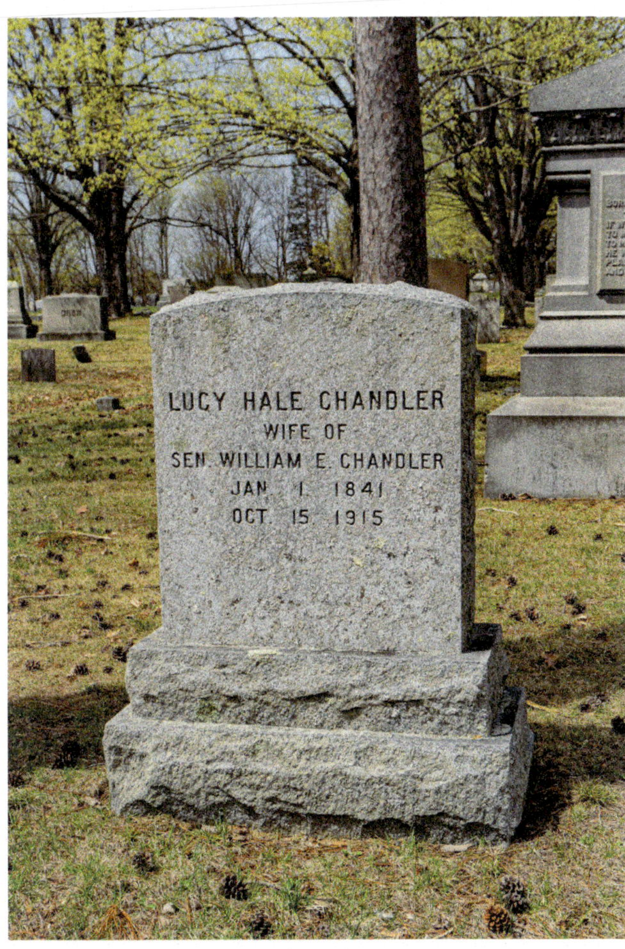

Grave of Lucy Hale; buried next to her husband.

Harriet Patience Dame (1815–1900), Blossom Hill Cemetery, Concord

At the outset of the war, Harriet Dame volunteered to serve as a matron or nurse to the 2nd New Hampshire Regiment. Governor National Berry denied her request, saying that the war was no place for a woman. She ignored him and went on to serve with the 2nd until it was mustered out of service in December 1865. Unlike many of the Civil War nurses who served in hospitals, Harriet insisted on being on the front line. From the regiment's first engagement at the First Battle of Bull Run, she was in the thick of it, evacuating the wounded and tending to their wounds. Gilman Marston, commander of the 2nd New Hampshire Regiment, later wrote of her:

> Miss Dame was the bravest woman I ever knew. I have seen her face a battery without flinching while a man took refuge behind her to avoid the flying fragments of bursting shells. Of all the men and women who volunteered to serve their country during the late war, no one deserves reward more than Harriet P. Dame.

The men likened her to an angel of mercy and affectionately called her "Aunt Harriet." She was twice captured by the enemy and released. On the second occasion, she was accused of being a spy and threatened with being shot. General "Stonewall" Jackson intervened and had her returned to Union lines.

Her service to her country did not end with the war. She remained in Washington, D.C., working as a clerk for the Treasury Department. In 1887, she succeeded Dorothea Dix as the Army Nurses Association president. During her tenure, she campaigned tirelessly for the recognition of Civil War nurses. She never stopped giving. She donated funds to help finance the 2nd Regiment's Camp at what is now Weirs Beach, and she also gave funds to the construction of the Old Soldiers Home in Tilton, now the state's Veterans Hospital.

Harriet received many honors during and after her lifetime. Her portrait hangs in the State House in Concord; the first woman to be so honored. Governor Maggie Hassan proclaimed December 2015 as Harriet Patience Dame Month, commemorating the 200th anniversary of her birth. She is buried in Blossom Hill Cemetery in Concord. A special monument was commissioned by "Her Boys" to mark the sight. The diamond on the monument represents the cap badge of the 3rd Corps of the Army of the Potomac, of which the 2nd New Hampshire Regiment was a part.

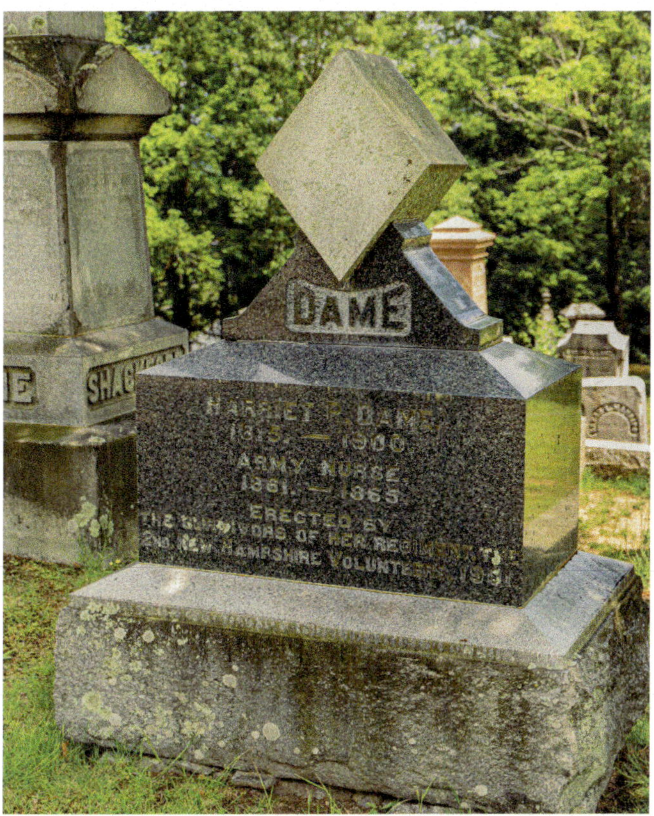

Grave of Harriet Dame.

Jeremiah Tabor (1782–1843), Indian Stream Republic, Indian Stream Cemetery, Pittsburg

After the American Revolutionary War, the Treaty of Paris in 1783 was unclear as to the exact borders between what is now Pittsburg, New Hampshire, and British-occupied Canada. The northwesternmost head of the Connecticut River was the designated boundary, but there were, due to tributaries, disagreements on how to interpret what that meant. The United States and Britain exercised their perceived rights over the territory by disputing local land titles, double taxation, and military conscription. By 1832, many of the approximately 300 inhabitants had had enough. Under the leadership of Justice of the Peace Luther Parker, Richard J. Blanchard, Jeremiah Tabor, Burley Blood, Abner Hyland, and William White, a constitution was drafted, and the independent Republic of Indian Stream was established between Indian Stream and Hall Stream. A monument to Jeremiah Tabor is prominent in the Indian Stream Cemetery. Abner Hyland lies in an unmarked grave. The others are apparently buried elsewhere. The leadership of the Republic, to avoid an invasion by a Coos County militia, agreed to be annexed by New Hampshire in 1835.

The British did not come through when requested for protection from such an invasion. Richard Blanchard was appointed deputy sheriff by the Coos County Sheriff. Not long after, Blanchard set out to arrest a man for not paying a hardware store debt. Blanchard's posse arrested the man who claimed he was illegally detained in Canada. British authorities issued a warrant for Blanchard's arrest. He was arrested but was freed by a group of undisciplined, drunken Indian Stream citizens. The British sheriff and magistrate were wounded. This time, a New Hampshire militia was sent to keep the peace. This created an international incident that led to an uneasy peace as neither the United States nor Britain wished to go to war over an unpaid hardware bill. In April 1836, the citizens of the Indian Stream Republic accepted a resolution granting complete control of the territory to New Hampshire. In 1838, the British gave up their claim to the territory. The Indian Stream Republic was incorporated as the town of Pittsburg in 1840. The international boundary was recognized in 1842 by the Webster-Ashburton Treaty. Pittsburg is a favorite fishing destination for both Bill and me.

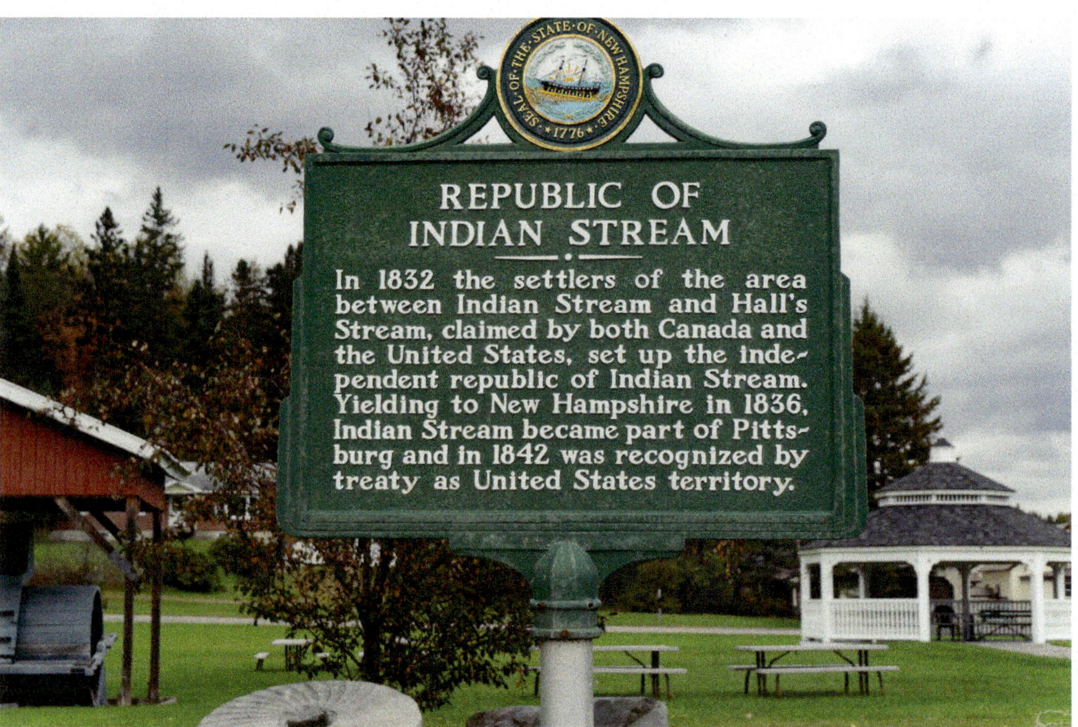

Historical marker, Pittsburg.

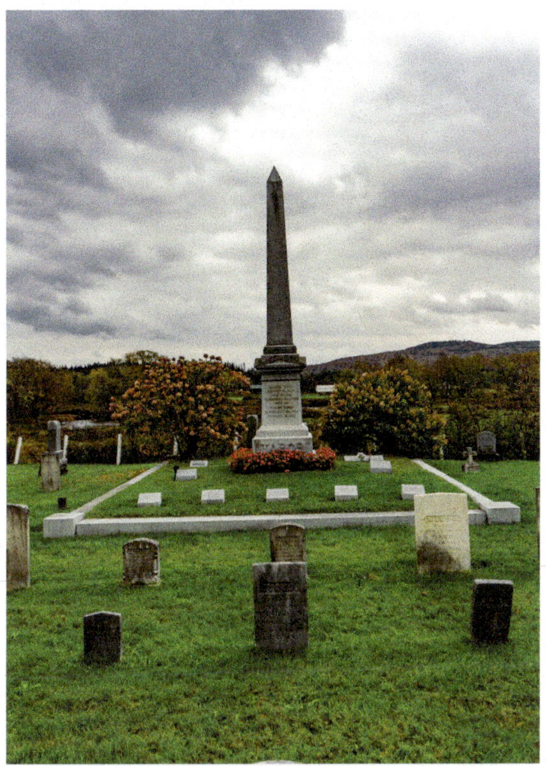

Right: Jeremiah Tabor, Indian Stream
Cemetery, Pittsburg.

Below: Historical tablet, Indian Stream
Cemetery, Pittsburg.

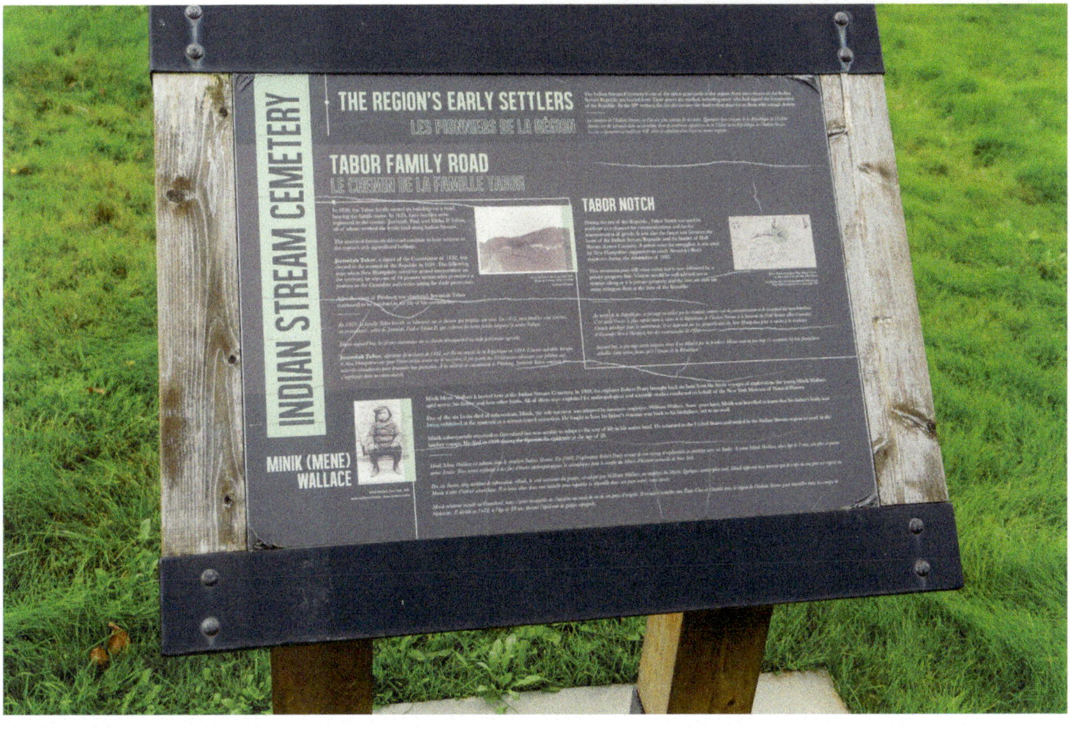

Doctor Ester Hill Hawks (1833–1906) and Doctor John M. Hawks (1826–1910), Pine Grove Cemetery, Manchester

The State of New Hampshire sent nearly 40,000 men to fight in the Civil War; among them were a handful of remarkable women who served as nurses and doctors. Doctor Ester Hawks served as a nurse and a doctor alongside her husband, John Hawks. Ester was born in Hooksett in 1833 and married her husband, John, in 1854. Soon after her marriage, she became interested in medicine and began to read her husband's medical books. Much to her husband's chagrin, she entered the New England Female Medical College in Boston and graduated from there as a doctor in 1857. John is said to have bemoaned the decision and wished she had spent more time attending to him than her studies. Ester and John were staunch abolitionists and, at the outset of the Civil War, volunteered their services in the Union Cause. The army refused to allow female surgeons in the service. When she volunteered as a nurse, she was turned down by Dorothea Dix, superintendent of army nurses, because she was too young and attractive and, therefore, would be a distraction.

John was no less the powerhouse that Ester was, and together, they were destined to further the cause of African Americans in the South. Aside from his medical practice, he was an author, teacher, newspaper publisher, army officer, school superintendent, and clerk of the Florida House. In 1861, John volunteered to treat escaped slaves in South Carolina and established a school for their children. He strongly advocated for black troops in the Civil War and helped raise the 33rd Colored Troops and joined the unit as their surgeon, being commissioned a major. He later held the same position with the 21st Colored Troops. He established a hospital for black soldiers in Beaufort, South Carolina. He was joined by his wife, Ester, who served as a surgeon's assistant. Here, John and Ester treated the wounded of the famed 54th Massachusetts Volunteer Infantry Regiment after the ill-fated attack on Fort Wagner, which was made famous in the movie *Glory*. When John was transferred to the 21st Colored Troops in Jacksonville, Ester went with him. In Jacksonville, Ester started the first integrated school in Florida.

Ester is buried in Pine Grove Cemetery in Manchester in her family's plot. The large stone is inscribed with her husband's name and his connection to the 33rd and 21st Colored Troops. Ester's favorite motto is inscribed under her name: "On the proper training of the children rests the hope of the world." Ester might have passed into obscurity had it not been for her diary being discovered in an attic in 1975. It was published under the name *A Woman Doctor's Civil War Diary*, edited by Gerald Schwartz. It is still in print.

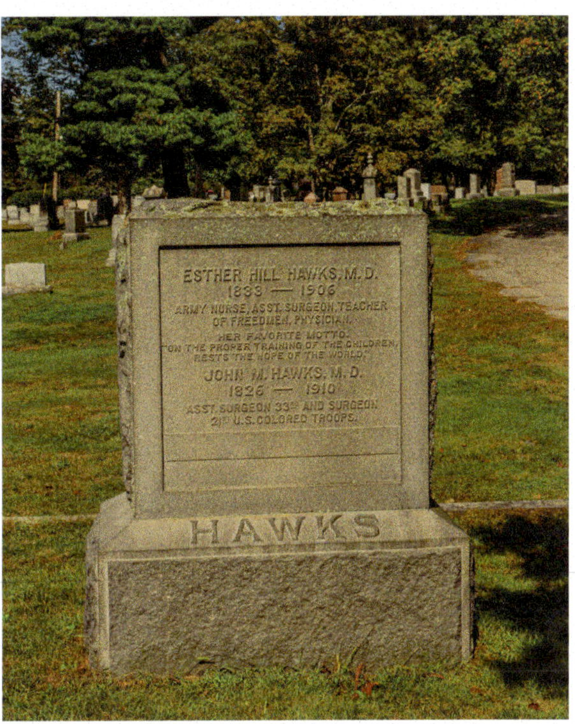

Grave of Esther Hawks.

Chinook Kennels Arthur Treadwell Walden (1871–1947), Milton John Seeley (1891–1943), Eva "Short" Seeley (1891–1985), Dick Moulton (1917–2000), Union Chapel, Wonalancet, Jewell Cemetery, Albany

The small village of Wonalancet once played a significant role in sled dog breeding. After spending time in Alaska during the gold rush, sled dog driver Arthur Treadwell Walden bred a mastiff and a Greenland husky to create the Chinook breed. Walden founded the kennels bearing the same name and was the lead sled driver and dog trainer for the 1928 Admiral Byrd expedition to Antarctica. This unique American breed was known for its strength, pulling ability, and gentleness. It can be traced genetically to one dog, Chinook, who became a celebrity in the dog sled world and beyond. Chinook and Walden led the first dog sled team up Mt. Washington. Chinook unfortunately died during the trip to Antarctica. The Chinook Trail, the road between Tamworth and Wonalancet, was to be named after Walden, but he insisted that it honor the legendary Chinook. Walden sold the Kennels to Milton and Eva Seeley, who carried on the Chinook bloodline along with others, such as Siberian huskies. They bred dogs for arctic expeditions, racing, and show, and for the U.S. Army during World War II. Milton died in 1943, and "Short," as Eva was known, carried on as a significant player in dog racing, breeding, and writing. She was inducted into the Mushers Hall of Fame in Alaska. The now-rare Chinook breed is the official breed of New Hampshire.

A friend of the Seeley's Richard, "Dick" Moulton, also made a name for himself as a sled dog racer. He reputedly won the prestigious Laconia World Championship more times than any other racer. He accompanied Byrd on his third expedition to Antarctica. During World War II, Sgt. Moulton participated in search and rescue missions in Labrador. Highly respected dog racing outfitter Ed Moody said that Dick was "The finest driver, the person who could get the most performance out of a team." Richard Moulton lies buried at the entrance of the old Chinook Kennels. The Seeleys are in the Jewel Cemetery in Albany near Wonalancet. Walden is at the Wonalancet Union Chapel.

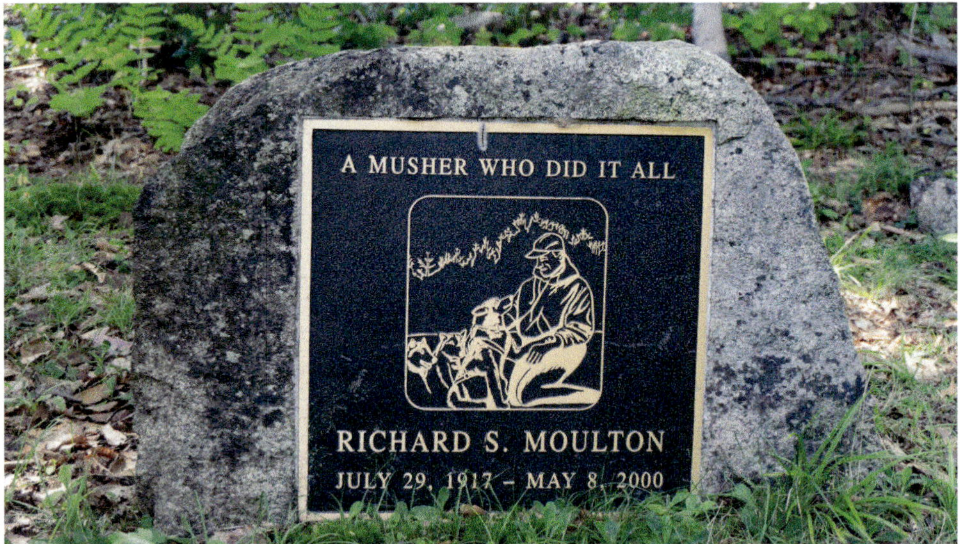

Above: Richard S. Moulton marker.

Below: Admiral Byrd Memorial.

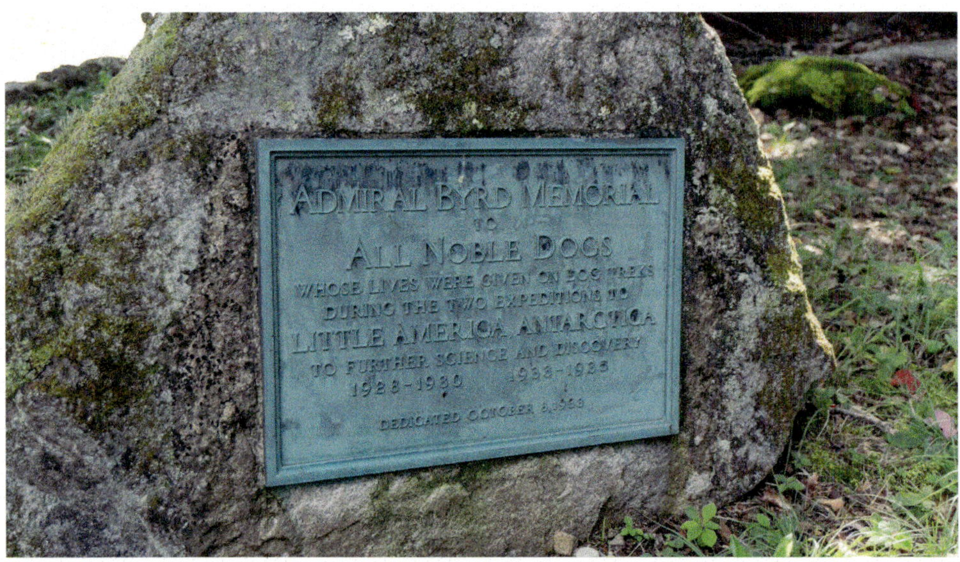

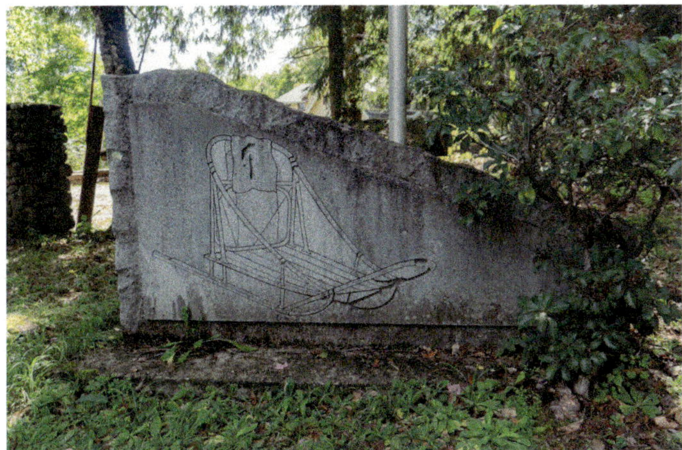

Dog sled.

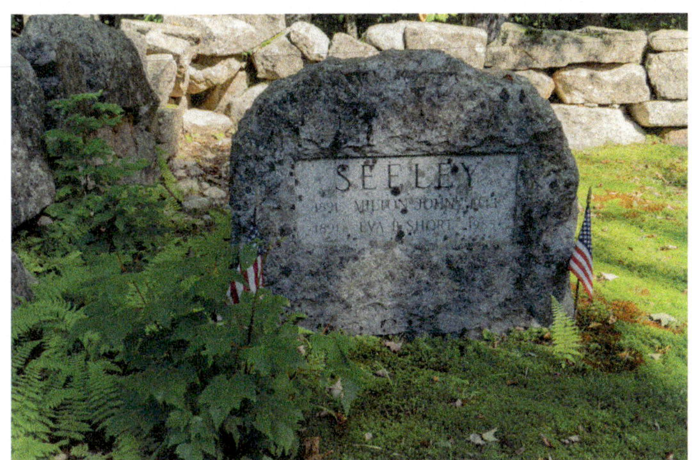

Milton John Seeley and Eva "Short" Seeley's grave.

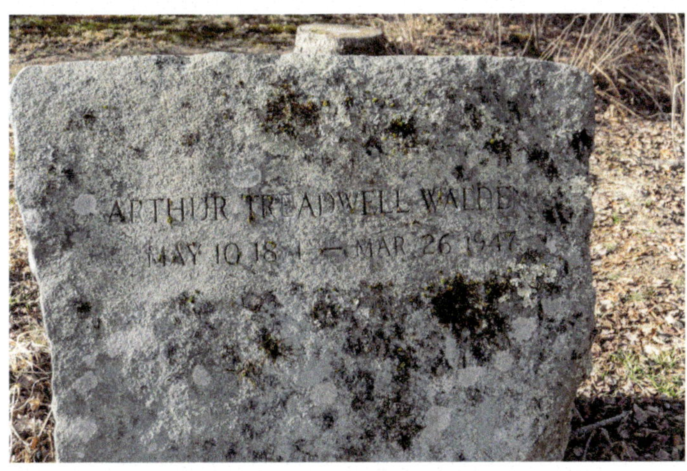

Arthur Treadwell Walden's grave.

Jigger Johnson (1871–1935), North Conway

The Jigger Johnson Campground is popular on the well-known scenic Kancamagus Highway. As a kid growing up in Conway, I heard stories about the legend Albert Lewis (Jigger) Johnson. I researched him for this book, but much of what I am about to relate is the stuff of local lore. I had to convince Bill that this long-dead logger deserved our attention. Some said Jigger was born wearing logging boots, holding an ax, chewing tobacco, or smoking a pipe. Jigger himself admitted that his reputation was a bit exaggerated. He claimed, though, that he "could run faster, jump higher, squat lower, move sideways quicker, and spit further than any son-of-bitch in camp." The truer exploits come from his good friend Dartmouth College Forester Bob Monahan.

Monahan helped found the Mt. Washington Observatory. While Jigger might have seemed like a big man, he was only 5 feet 6 inches tall and weighed 160 pounds. Those pounds were all muscle, and Monahan praised Jigger for his "head full of brains." Albert Johnson was born in Fryeburg, Maine, presumably with no tobacco products in his mouth. By age twelve, Johnson worked as a cook's helper at a logging camp. This is where the legend begins. Conversation during dinner was forbidden at the camp. Johnson took it upon himself to defend this tradition when some drunk loggers became boisterous. Johnson asked the rugged men to be silent. One of the men pushed the "cookee" to the ground. This was a mistake as Johnson fought back by jumping on the drunk and biting off part of his ear. After the fight, the other loggers passed the hat to buy Johnson a new shirt and a pound of chewing tobacco. By twenty, Johnson was a head chopper at a camp on the Androscoggin River. His reputation grew. As a logger and a woodsman, few men were his equal. It wasn't a tall tale that he could sleep in the snow, survive in the winter by eating tree bark, and catch bobcats with his bare hands. He could fell a tree with absolute precision, but he was just as famous for his ability to drink prodigious amounts of alcohol and drunken brawls. Once the pulpwood was no longer profitable, Jigger took on other work. On sunny days, he was respected and effective as a trail builder and an amiable fire watcher on Mount Chocorua and Carter Dome. Assuming he wasn't needed on rainy days, he would be drawn to any form of alcohol. He was fired from one job because his still caught fire. Next, he went on to work with the Civilian Conservation Corps during the Depression. He was successful at training new CCC workers by sharing his skills as a woodsman.

The CCC had rules that included shaving, bathing, and studying. This didn't suit him, so Jigger moved on and spent his final years as a trapper living in a cabin in Passaconaway. Respecting a New Hampshire law that traps had to be inspected within twenty-four hours after being set, Johnson hired a driver to take him from Conway to Passaconaway. He had been in Conway celebrating a lynx pelt sale. The car slid off the icy road, pinning the indestructible living legend against a tree just as Jigger exited the vehicle. He died soon after, on March 30, 1935, at Memorial Hospital in North Conway. Who knows how many of the tall tales about Jigger Johnson were true? True or not, Jigger Johnson lived large in an era that no longer exists. Where Jigger is buried remains a mystery to us.

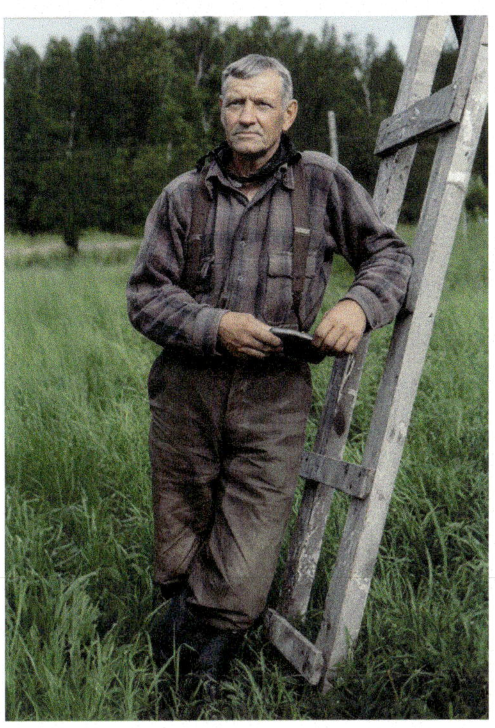

Photo of Jigger Johnson. (*Public Domain*)

Old Aggie (1740–1840), Pine Grove Cemetery, Barrington

Outside the entrance to the Pine Grove Cemetery in Barrington is New Hampshire State Historical Highway Marker No. 279. It was placed there at the request of the Barrington Historical Society and the First Congregational Church of Barrington to commemorate the town's 300th anniversary. The marker notes the Reverand Balch family plot and the grave of Old Aggie. The Reverand Benjamin Balch was the first chaplain of the Continental Navy and later the pastor of the Congregational Church; he died in 1815. Old Aggie was an African Slave brought to Barrington in 1740. Aggie is thought to be the last slave to die in New Hampshire.

New Hampshire never had a large population of slaves. However, it did play a prominent role in bringing slaves into the colonies. Many prominent families of Portsmouth grew rich off the triangle trade. New Hampshire had the unique position of having no tariff on the importation of slaves. Despite some vague wording in the state's constitution of "all men being equal" and a very strong abolitionist movement, slavery did not end in New Hampshire until the Thirteenth Amendment was passed in 1865.

Aggie was brought to Barrington at the age of eleven by Captain Mark Hunking and, upon his death, was moved to the Balch family, with whom she lived until her passing in 1840. Although her birth date is unknown, she lived to be over 100. At some point, she had been emancipated by the Balch family. She was well loved by the Barrington community. She was said to have been kind and known for caring for the sick. In 1932, the Daughters of the American Revolution had Aggie moved to the Balch family plot in Pine Grove Cemetery. Even at that late date, the people of Barrington still remembered her fondly.

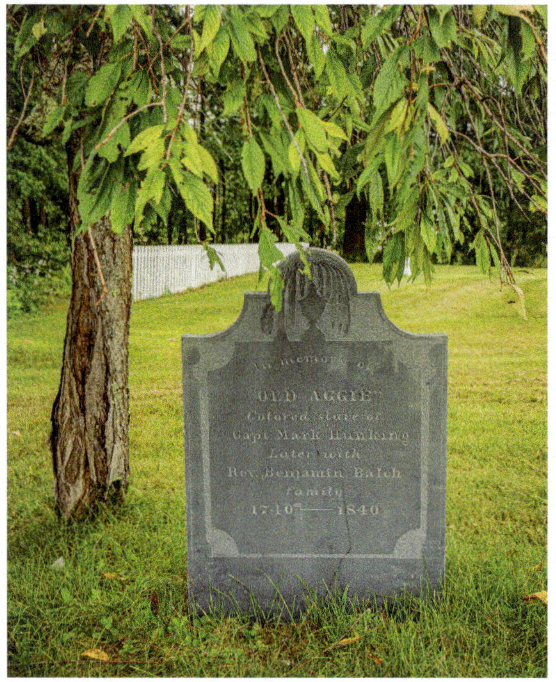

Resting place of Old Aggie.

Metallak (died c. 1850), "The Lone Indian of the Magalloway," North Hill Cemetery, Stewartstown

There is conflicting information on Metallak's life. The following is the stuff of legend and may not be historically accurate, but nonetheless fascinating. He was a chief and the son of a chief of the Coo-ash-auke Indians. It is said that he lived to be 120 years old. Most of his tribe had disappeared, perhaps from disease. As a youth, Metallak may have resisted the coming of the white man, but later, after a vision from the Great Spirit, he lived in peace with the invading Europeans. He even aided them in adapting to their new world. Metallak was known as a highly skilled hunter and warrior. Metallak's territory was the northern parts of New Hampshire and northwestern Maine. Metallak may have served in the U.S. Army in the War of 1812. He certainly assisted the white man, but he never turned his back on his native heritage. He supported himself in traditional ways until he was too old to do so. He was known for his aversion to farming and preferred to live from hunting and trapping. He was highly regarded by both his own people and the white settlers. Metallak's first wife, Keoka, was said to be very beautiful but sadly died at a young age. Metallak and Keoka had lost their first child to wolves. After that, Metallak took revenge on every wolf he encountered. According to those who knew him, Molly Oozalluc, Metallak's second wife, was not as beautiful as his first, but Metallak was deeply in love with her. He was heartbroken when Molly died. It may not have been uncommon in those times to preserve a body in the winter by smoking it. The body could be properly buried in the spring. Legend tells us that Metallak performed this ritual on his beloved wife. Some stories say he ultimately buried his wife on the Narrows of Richardson Lake in Maine; others say he interred her near Moll's Rock on Lake Umbagog, which is on the New Hampshire–Maine border. In any case, Oozalluc's resting place is a well-kept secret. A sacred place that was known only to Molly Oozalluc's adoring husband. In his younger years, Metallak was renowned for his survival skills, but later in life, he was disabled and impoverished because of blindness. He lost the vision in one eye while using a needle to sew a moccasin. He later lost his other eye in an accident while gathering wood.

The citizens of Stewartstown accepted the old man as a town pauper. His basic needs were provided for until he died and was buried in North Hill Cemetery in Stewartstown, just off Route 145. For many years, the cemetery was difficult to find unless you knew someone local to point the way. Today, there is a New Hampshire Historical Marker on Route 145. Recently, a local artist added a hand-carved sign pointing the way. Another recent addition is an ornamental fence on the gate with the likeness of Metallak. Metallak's stone was erected by John Emerson in 1915. Visitors to the site often leave tokens of respect on the grave.

The real resting place of Metallak is most likely in the right-hand corner of the cemetery, which served as the pauper's section. North Hill Cemetery is as beautiful as one will find in New Hampshire. Several Civil War veterans and at least one Revolutionary War veteran is buried in the cemetery.

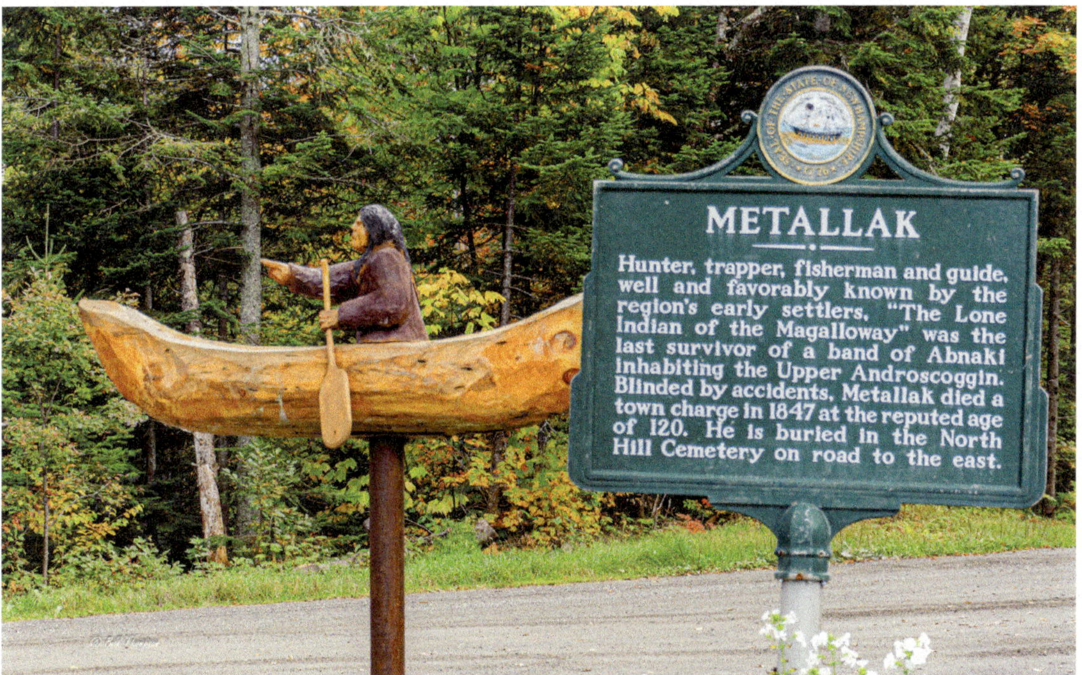

Metallak historical marker.

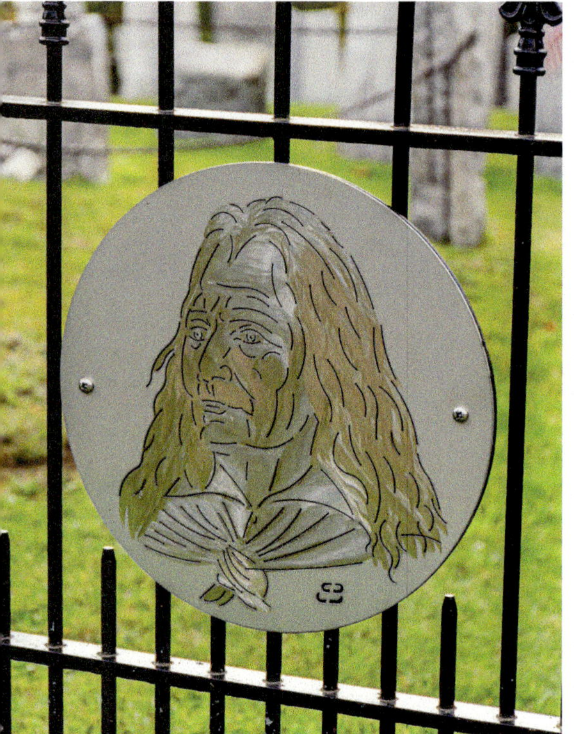

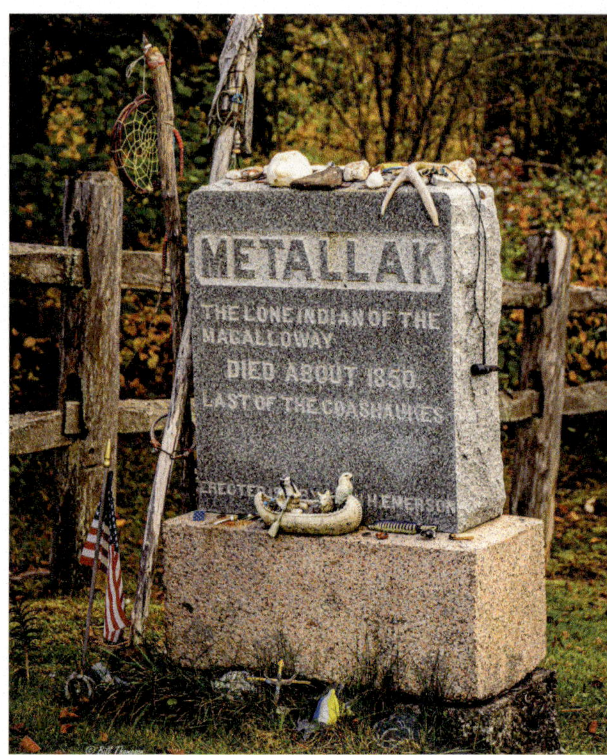

Above left: Fence at North Hill Cemetery, Stewartstown.

Above right: Grave of Metallak.

Captain John Lovewell (1621–1725), Fryeburg, Maine

John Lovewell was one of New England's most well-known militia captains during his time. Today, he is best known for his final battle in 1725, which ended with his death in Fryeburg, Maine. Chief Paugus, the leader of the Abenaki tribe, was also killed along with an unknown number of tribal warriors. Lovewell set out with forty-six scalp hunters; only twenty returned from the battle, three of whom died on the way home. Ten men had been left at a fort in Ossipee, NH. This turned out to be a decisive battle as it marked the end of the conflict between the Abenaki and the settlers. The importance of that for the settlers was commemorated by such authors as Henry Wadsworth Longfellow and Nathaniel Hawthorne. There is a memorial for the rangers who died that can be found on Lovewell Pond Road in Fryeburg, Maine. Today, Lovewell Pond is a popular place for summer residents to spend their vacations. After an ambush in Old Dunstable, NH, a militia of scalp hunters, under the leadership of Captain John Lovewell, was formed to address the perceived threat of other raids. A £1,000 bounty was to be paid for each scalp. Before the final expedition to Fryeburg, two other expeditions occurred in New Hampshire. One led north to Lake Winnipesaukee, where one scalp was taken. The second was near what is now Wakefield and led to the death of ten natives. Scalps were taken, and the skirmish was interpreted as successful in preventing a possible attack. The rangers returned as heroes and proudly paraded around, displaying the scalps they had taken. Captain Lovewell wore headgear made of scalps. The rangers demonstrating proof of their victory were even celebrated in Boston. There is a state marker in Ossipee near the Indian Mound commemorating Lovewell's campaigns. Bill and I haven't found reliable evidence that the Indian Mound is a Native American burial ground. The times were harsh for the New England Colonists and the Wabanaki Confederation during what was known by some as Captain Lovewell's War (Wabanaki–New England War).

> *The din of the battle, the tumult, is o'er,*
> *And the war-clarion's voice is now heard no more.*

Longfellow

"Roger Malvin's Burial" is a short story referring to Lovewell's Battle by Nathaniel Hawthorne

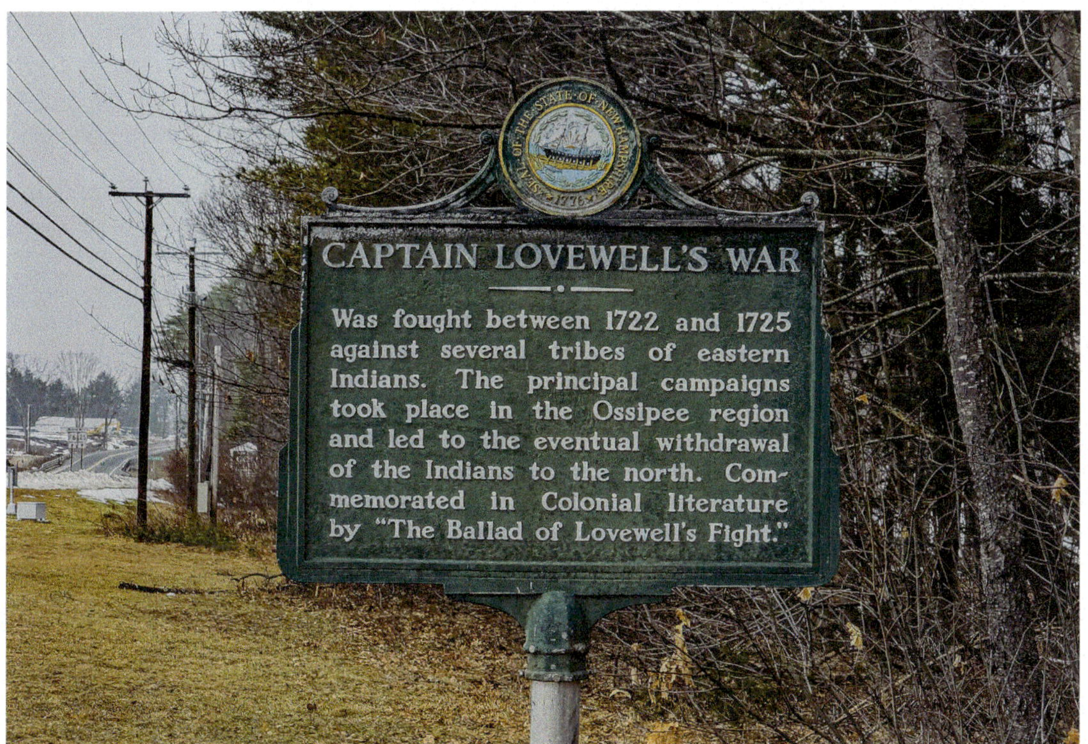

Captain John Lovewell historical marker in Ossipee.

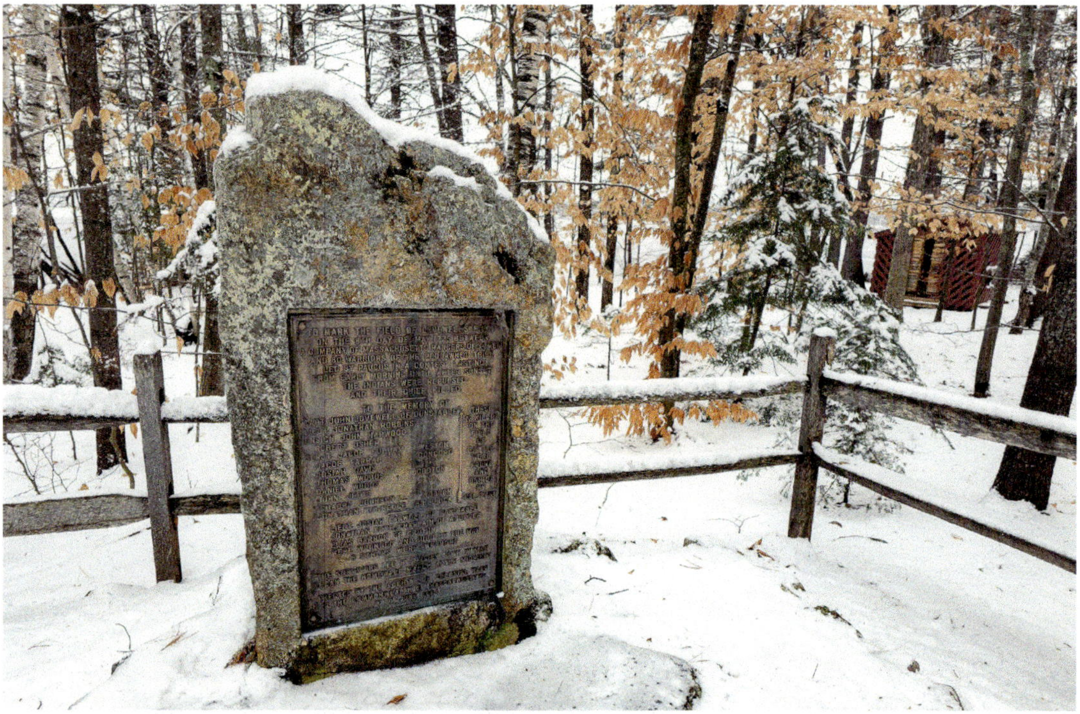

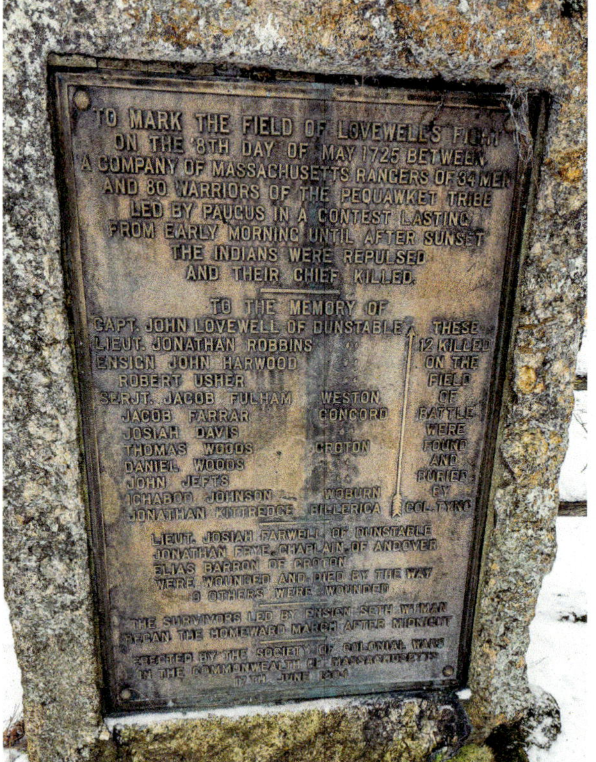

Above: Memorial of the Battle on Lovewell Pond, Fryeburg, Maine.

Left: Detail of the Lovewell Memorial.

Samuel Hidden (1760–1837), Tamworth Cemetery

Just outside Tamworth Village on Cleveland Hill Road is an obelisk on top of a glacial boulder. This boulder is known as Ordination Rock. The obelisk memorializes Reverend Samuel Hidden, ordained as Tamworth's first permanent minister on the rock in 1792. The following is from Reverend Hidden's memoir:

> is a large rock about thirty feet square and
> fifteen feet high. The surface is almost
> level. On this it was resolved that Mr.
> Hidden should be ordained, since there was
> no Meeting House

According to Hidden, people came from all around, dressed in their best clothing, to witness this event. The reverend had come to provide spiritual guidance to all. He served as pastor of the Congregational Church in Tamworth for forty-six years. He was a graduate of Dartmouth College. As an ardent supporter of independence, he enlisted in the Revolutionary War four times. He had to go. Fighters for the cause were bleeding on the battlefield. Reverend Hidden was more than a spiritual leader. He taught music, formed a choir, and involved himself in the local schools, some of which he founded. Samuel started one of the first libraries in New Hampshire. He also wrote a memoir. It is a fascinating read as the book reveals the thoughts and experiences of an educated and talented man of his time. *The Memoir of Reverend Samuel Hidden* can be found online. It has also been republished but remains in the public domain. Samuel Hidden's grandson arranged for the erection of the obelisk in 1862. There are stone steps that lead up to the top of the rock, so you can stand where Reverend Hidden once stood. He is buried across the street. The memorial resembles a large table. The inscriptions on the obelisk read:

> Memorial of the Ordination on this ROCK, September 12, 1792, of the Rev. SAMUEL HIDDEN as Pastor of the Congregational Church Instituted on that day.

> Born in Rowley, Mass, February 22, 1760.
> Served in the War of the Revolution by four Enlistments 1777-1781.
> Graduated at Dart. College, 1791.
> Minister in Tamworth 46 years died February 13, 1837, AEt. 77.

> He came into the Wilderness and left it a Fruitful field.
> To perpetuate the memory of his virtues and Public Services a Grandson, bearing his honored name Provided for the erection of this Cenotaph, 1862.

The base contains the following information: "Town Charted 1766, Settled in 1771, 40 families, Census of 1860, 1717."

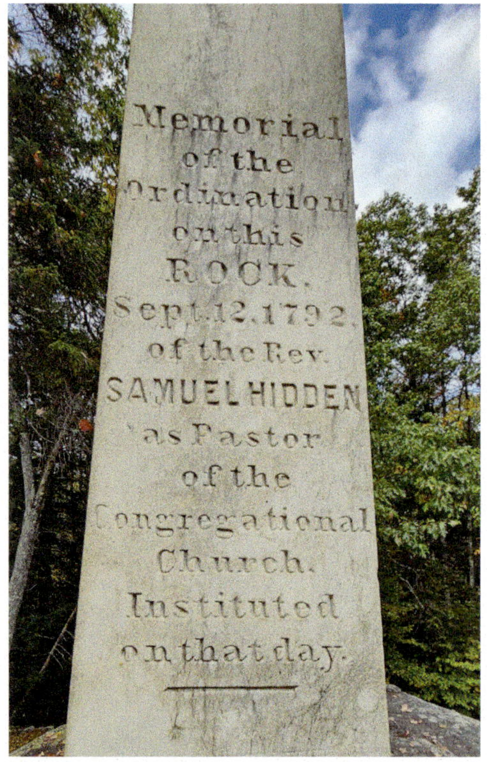

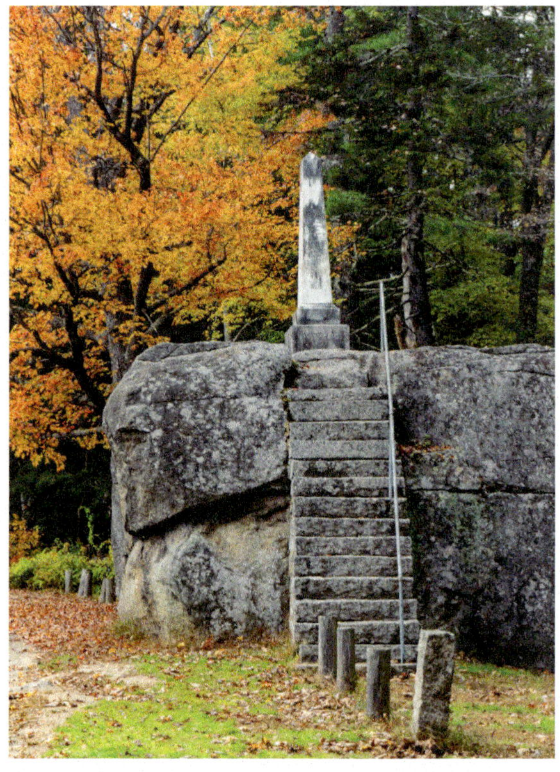

Above left: Monument on Ordination Rock, Tamworth.

Above right: Ordination Rock.

Left: Samuel Hidden's grave in the Tamworth Town Cemetery.

3
CELEBRITIES

Grace Metalious (1924–1964), Smith Cemetery, Gilmanton

Grace Metalious's *Peyton Place* was one of the bestselling novels ever. At its publication in 1956, it was also one of the most scandalous. The book wasn't well received by critics but certainly was by readers worldwide. By today's standards, the book seems relatively tame, but it does depict the "dirty laundry" of a small town. Grace had lived in Belmont and finally in Gilmanton, both small villages, much like many others in New Hampshire. How much of the story reflected reality is debatable. The murder in the book is, indeed, based on actual events. Notably, the novel is about women and was published by a woman. It was also about wealth, poverty, hypocrisy, and sex. Unsurprisingly, there were those in the town who were upset with Grace's portrayal of what was assumed to be Gilmanton.

Success did not make Grace Metalious a happy woman. She struggled with relationships, alcohol, writing her subsequent novels, and went through all the royalties from her bestseller and from the films based on her book. When Bill and I visited Grace's grave in Smith Cemetery in Gilmanton, there was an empty plastic bottle of Fireball. Appropriate, it would seem. Filmmaker John Waters left a bottle of booze at some point, maybe Seagram's 7, her favorite whiskey. That's gone. There are coins on the grave left by those who still feel an affinity for her writing and life. We contributed. I recently read *Peyton Place* and found it better written than I expected. Metalious' description of the town meeting was spot on. She did expose those things you are only supposed to whisper about behind 1950's closed doors.

The opening line of *Peyton Place*: "Indian summer is like a woman. Ripe, hotly passionate, but fickle, she comes and goes as she pleases so that one is never sure whether she will come at all, nor for how long she will stay."

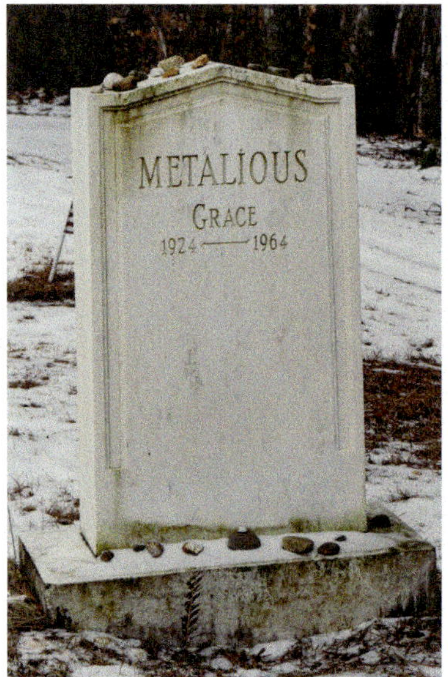

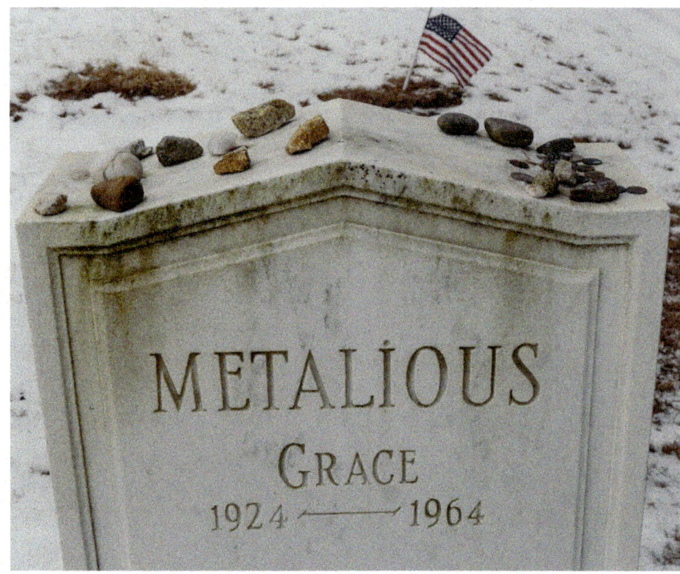

Above left: Lone grave of Grace Metalious; Grace purchased surrounding lots to rest eternally alone.

Above right: Grave goods on Grace Metalious' grave.

Tammy Grimes (1934–2016), Great Hill Cemetery, Chester

Tammy Grimes was an award-winning theater and film actress. She is best known for her role on Broadway as Molly, the famous *Titanic* survivor, in *The Unsinkable Molly Brown*. She won a Tony Award for this performance and one for her role as Amanda Prynne in Noel Coward's *Private Lives*. She worked several times with Noel Coward, a famous English playwright, actor, singer, song composer, and director. She had her own television program and appearances on such TV classics as *Mr. Broadway* and *Route 66*. When Coward died in 1973, Grimes was given the honor of being the first celebrity to lay flowers on his memorial statue in Manhattan. In 1965, Tammy made the news as she was attacked and injured twice in four days, allegedly by white supremacists, because she worked with black entertainers. She had recently made public appearances with Sammy Davis Jr. She was initially chosen to play Samantha on the successful TV show *Bewitched* but turned the part down. Elizabeth Montgomery became a star playing the part, but Tammy Grimes was a star in her own right for roles on and off Broadway, in films, and on TV. She was inducted into the American Theater Hall of Fame in 2003. Quite a career, and she now rests in the town of Chester. Bill and I visited her grave in the winter. We found the family headstone, but Tammy's was buried in snow.

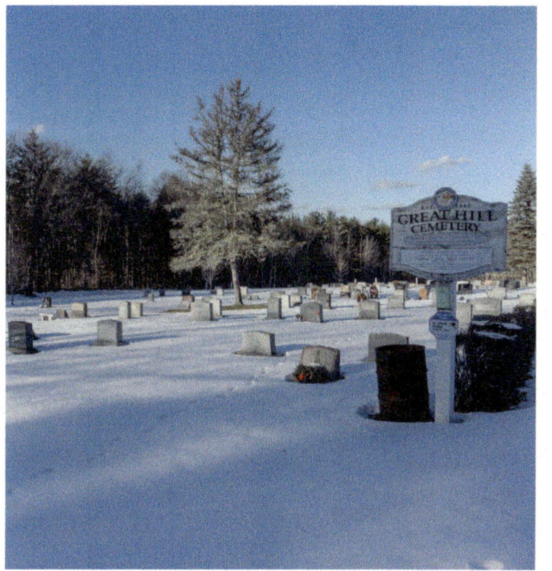

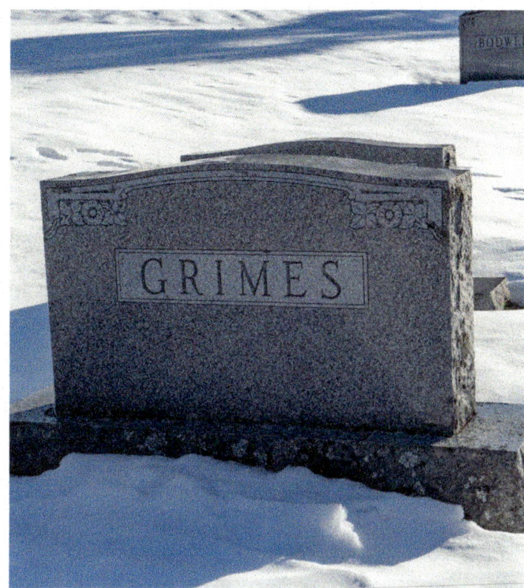

Above left: Great Hill Cemetery, Chester.

Above right: Grimes family stone.

Tommy Makem (1932–2007), New St, Mary Cemetery, Dover

Tommy Makem, the godfather of Irish music, may have been born in Northern Ireland, but he later made his home in Dover, New Hampshire. He is buried there. The Clancy Brothers and Tommy Makem were one of the most well-known folk groups during the folk era in the late 1950s and 1960s. This was the time of such groups as the Kingston Trio, Peter Paul and Mary, the Limelighters, the Brothers Four, and New Hampshire's Brandywine Singers. The Clancy's and Makem stuck to their roots as Irish singers. Makem was usually seen playing a long-neck five-string banjo, but he also mastered the tin whistle, low whistle, bagpipes, bodhran, and guitar. He was a poet and songwriter known for storytelling and a keen, if somewhat silly, sense of humor. Northern Irish folk singer Sarah Makem was Tommy's mother, who married fiddler Peter Makem. The musical tradition is carried on today by Tommy's sons, the Makem Brothers.

Familiar songs from the Clancy Brothers and Tommy Makem include "The Rising of the Moon," "Irish Rover," "Jug of Punch," "Four Green Fields," "Gentle Annie," and "Red is the Rose." Ultimately, there are too many to mention here. "Finnegan's Wake," an old traditional Irish song, apparently influenced well-known Irish author James Joyce. Tommy was awarded three honorary doctorates from the University of Limerick, the University of Ulster, and the University of New Hampshire. He received the Lifetime Achievement Award from the World Folk Music Association. There is a bridge over the Cocheco River

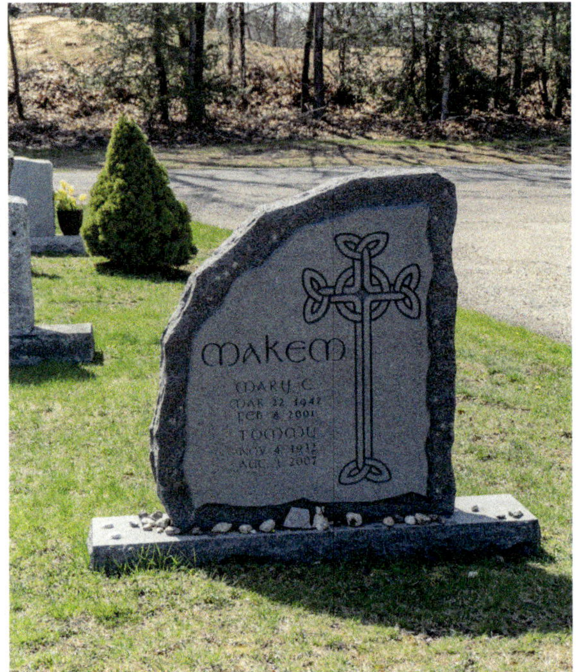

Grave of Tommy Makem.

in Dover named after Tommy and his wife, Mary. After visiting his gravesite, Bill and I have enjoyed listening to Tommy Makem's and the Clancy Brothers's songs. Tommy may have been Irish through and through, but New Hampshire can also claim him.

Shaw Brothers, Rick (1941–2021) and Ron (1941–2018), Freedom

The Shaw Brothers were a folk group that started out in Conway. They were six years ahead of me at Kennett High School, and as "a want-to-be folk singer" back then, I was impressed by their music. Folk music was popular during my junior high, high school, and college years. My first album was a Kingston Trio album. I listened to it for hours and learned to play all the trio songs and later those performed by Rick and Ron Shaw, among other folk acts. "I Want to Hold Your Hand" by the Beatles hit the USA in 1964, and Bob Dylan performed with an electric guitar at the Newport Folk Festival in 1965. Popular music tastes changed, but the Shaw Brothers continued the melodic folk tradition. I have always admired them for that. I turned to Bob Dylan, New Hampshire native Tom Rush, The Rolling Stones, and the blues, but I continued to follow Rick and Ron.

While in college at the University of New Hampshire, they performed as The Tradewinds and later The Brandywine Singers. They performed with the Hilltop Singers, a group that had a hit with "I'd Like to Teach the World to Sing." Ron performed with country legend Don Williams and Taylor Pie as part of the Pozo-Seco Singers while Rick served in Vietnam. They are remembered as the Shaw Brothers, "New Hampshire's

Ambassadors to the World." Their song "New Hampshire Naturally" is the official song of New Hampshire. I often love to bring out the Shaw Brothers' old and later albums when the mood hits me. I don't know how many times I saw them perform formally and informally. I can thank them for that when I get my guitar out; I still play some folk songs. We didn't know where to find their final resting place, but Ron's partner, Sallie Macintosh, told us where to find where their ashes were laid to rest.

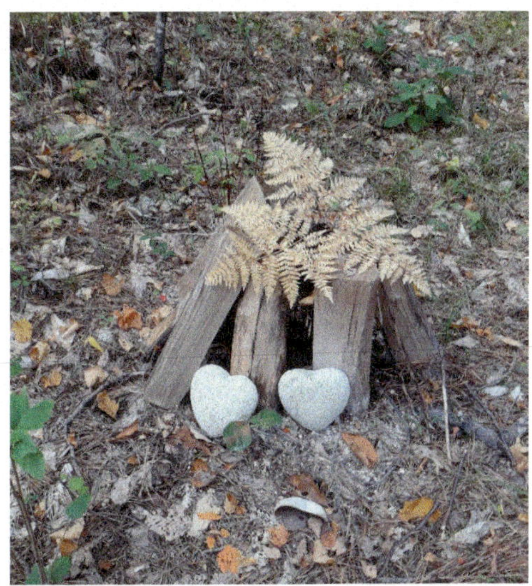

Right: Undisclosed site of Shaw Brothers in Freedom. (*Salie Macintosh Photo*)

Below: Shaw Brothers performing. (*Sallie Macintosh Photo*)

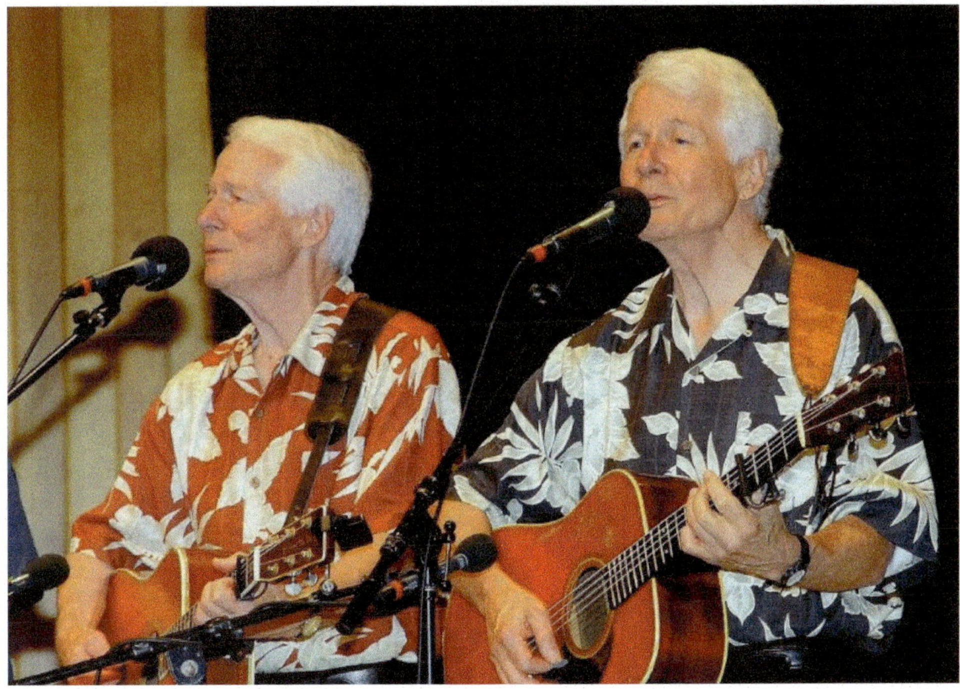

Hannes Schneider (1890–1955), Our Lady of the Mountains Catholic Cemetery, North Conway

If you grew up in the Conway area, as I did, you couldn't help but be familiar with names such as Hannes Schneider, his son Herbert, Carroll Reed, Harvey Dow Gibson, George Morton, and Dr. G. Harold Shedd, among others. Bill and I have found the graves of Hannes, Herbert Schneider, and Harvey Dow Gibson. All played integral roles in making skiing what it is today. Some would say modern skiing in New Hampshire started in 1934 when the Civilian Conservation Corps cut the first trail on Black Mountain in Bartlett. Ironically, a ski accident by local ski instructor Carroll Reed led to the next step in the evolution of skiing in North Conway and beyond. During nineteen weeks of recovery, while being treated by Dr. Schedd, Reed decided that an Austrian ski instructor should be brought to Jackson. With the arrival of Benno Rybizka, an American version of the Hannes Schneider Ski School was established. Franz Koessler, Otto Tschol, and Toni Matt soon followed. Matt is still famous today for his straight schuss down the Mount Washington Headwall in the American Inferno in 1939. In 1937, international financier Harvey Dow Gibson was looking to establish the ski industry to promote the economy of his native North Conway. He purchased Cranmore Mountain and what would become the Eastern Slope Inn. He engaged local mechanic George Morton to build a unique ski lift, the Skimobile.

A rope tow had served the mountain before that. In 1938, the snow trains arrived with skiers ready to ski in the Eastern Slopes Region. It was time to bring Hannes Schneider himself to New Hampshire. Schneider was an outspoken critic of the Nazi regime and was under house arrest in Germany. Since Germany still owed World War I war debt to one of Gibson's banks, a deal was struck with Heinrich Himmler to release Hannes Schneider and his family. The rest is local history. Cranmore was put on the map; Carroll Reed created the famous Carroll Reed Ski Shops, and Dr. Shedd became well-known and beloved as the "leg doctor." Hannes Schneider trained skiers in the legendary 10th Mountain Division during World War II. Herbert earned the Bronze Star for his service in the 10th in the campaign in Italy. The 10th Mountain Division was the only World War II army division specially trained to serve in the mountains, and its members served in Italy under some of the most challenging conditions during that war. They contributed to the German surrender in Italy.

I recommend *The History of Cranmore Mountain* by Tom Eastman for more on the intriguing history of this part of the state.

May Sarton ("My business is the analysis of feeling") (1912–1995), Nelson Cemetery, Nelson

I have always been attracted to books about living in isolated places, especially in northern New England. Many of the books in my collection are used, as I prefer to read original editions when possible. Many years ago, I picked up a signed first edition of May Sarton's *Journal of A Solitude*. I never got around to reading it, but it has been visible all these years, waiting for the right time. It was right there on the bookshelf next to my reading chair. The time has come. When Bill and I started looking for people to include in *Buried New Hampshire*, one of the first I thought of was May Sarton. Her journal

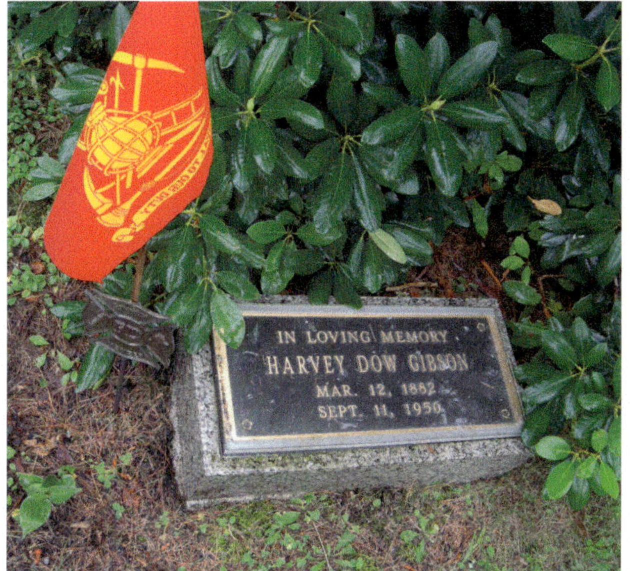

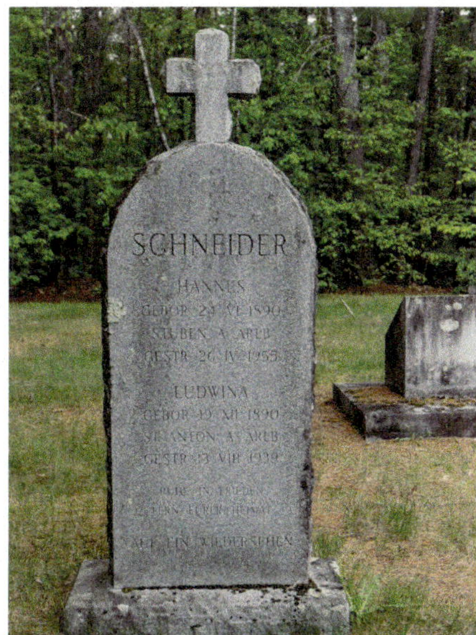

Above left: Grave of Harvey Dow Gibson.

Above right: Grave of Hannes Schneider.

about solitude was written in New Hampshire. I wondered whether the author was buried here. Her final resting place in Nelson is marked by one of the most unique memorials we have found: a sculpture of a phoenix. This work of art was sculptured and given to Sarton years before her death by a friend, sculptor Barbara Barton. After receiving the gift, May decided the phoenix was the suitable marker for her grave. The following is from her poem "The Phoenix Again": "The Phoenix takes its rest forgetting all desire." May says, "It (the phoenix) does just what I wanted, gives a sense of uprush of flight."

The memorial sits a little away from others. This seems very appropriate. May Sarton's poetry, novels, and journals speak of and reflect on the value of independence and solitude and the necessity of, but the inherent difficulty of, relationships. *The Fur Person* is a story of a stray cat, Tom Jones's search for a home. Sarton admired and identified with a cat's ability to be itself and not give up its independence while living among human beings. May Sarton was an introspective observer of the human condition. She wrote openly and honestly about inner emotions, depression, solace in nature, respect for simple rural lifestyles, gardens, challenges inherent in relationships, aging, being and valuing your true self, and sexuality. Mary was an open lesbian who advocated for women's rights. By her own admission, she could be a difficult person. According to her biographer, Margot Peters, "May Sarton was a complex individual who often struggled in her relationships. I have taken *A Journal of A Solitude* off the shelf and am happy that I have done so.

"We have to dare to be ourselves, however frightening or strange that self may prove to be."—Mary Sarton

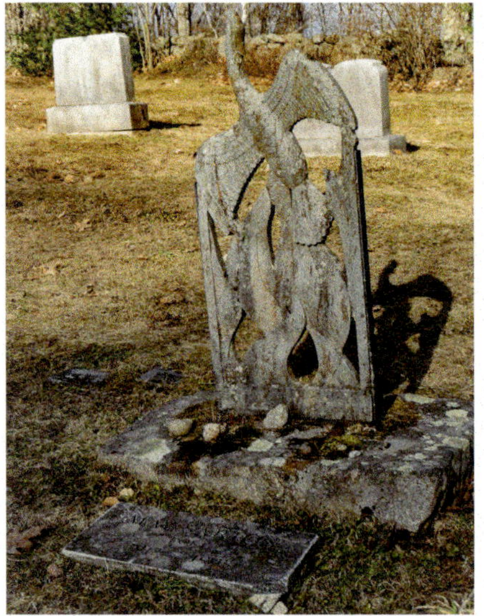

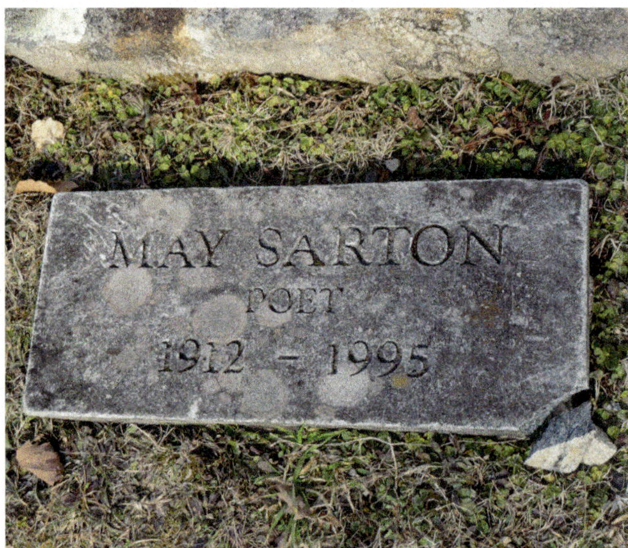

Above left: Grave of Mry Sarton.

Above right: Headstone of May Sarton.

Robert Lowell (1917–1977), Stark Cemetery, Dunbarton

Talking about the past is like a cat's trying to explain climbing down a ladder.

"Words in Air"

The quotation above sums up writing about such a complicated man as Robert Lowell. He was a poet. He was born to a famous family of means and historical significance, but he was rebellious. He left Harvard to go to Kenyon. He became a Catholic and later renounced that. He served time in prison as a conscientious objector during World War II. He refused to visit the Lyndon Johnson White House because he didn't think America was living up to its ideals. He participated in anti-war demonstrations but didn't see himself as political. He received, among many other awards, two Pulitzer Prizes. His poetry was confessional in that, as with his one-time student Sylvia Plath, his verse reflected his own life intimacies and suffering from bipolar disease. These were extreme. His highs were manic, and his depressions were deep. Lowell saw himself as split between "conscience" and "instinct." He didn't believe that artistic talent was something that could be taught. His intrinsic art often expressed the remorse and need to repair the damage done during times of severe depression. He saw the use of metaphor in his writing as his salvation. Many critics regarded Lowell as the best poet of his generation. John Berryman, a close friend and fellow poet, said, "A man who taught us that even in adversity, there is beauty to be found."

Through his mental illness, Lowell suffered multi-faceted adversity. Lowell shared the insights gained from this honestly, openly, and profoundly. When Bill and I visited Robert Lowell's grave in Dunbarton, we were surprised that he was buried in the Stark Cemetery among many of the descendants of General John Stark. There is some irony to the fact that in death, Lowell did not escape his connection to an illustrious New England past that he often expressed contempt for.

His grave is inscribed with the following:

> The Immortal is scraped unconsenting from the Mortal,
> We feel the machine slipping from our hands
> As if someone else was steering it;
> If we see light at the end of the tunnel,
> It is the light of an oncoming train.

"Skunk Hour"

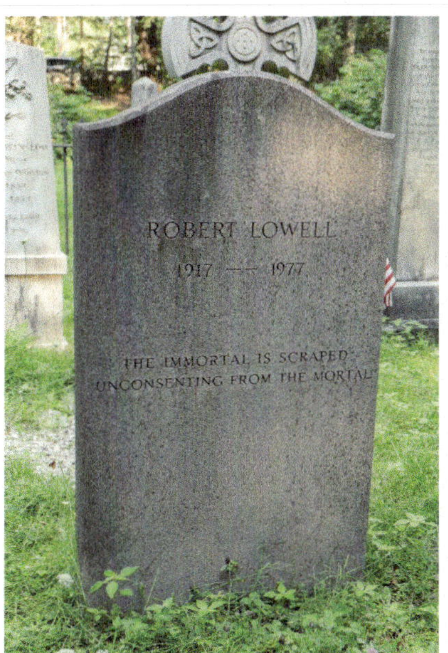

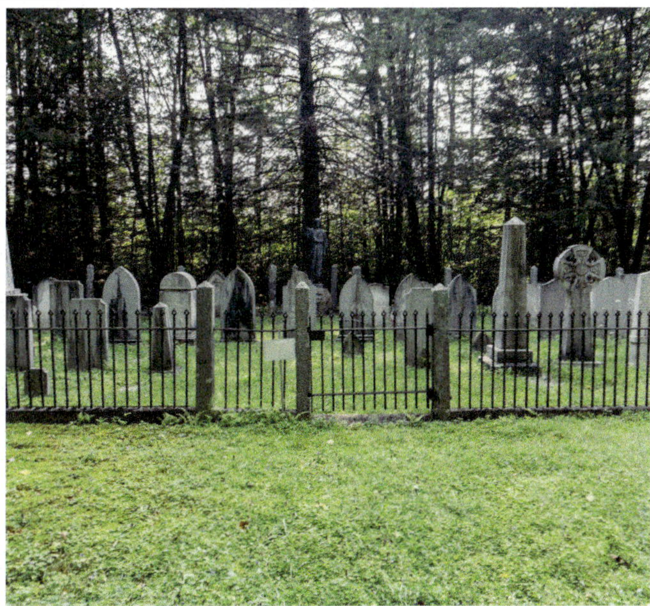

Above left: Grave of Robert Lowell.

Above right: Stark Cemetery, Dunbarton Center.

Jack Sharkey (1902–1994), Prospect Cemetery, Epping

Jack Sharkey was a famous American boxer who was the heavyweight champion on several occasions during the 1920s and 1930s. Born in 1902 as Joseph Paul Zukauskas in New York, he took his professional name from his two heroes, Jack Dempsey and Tom Sharkey. During his career, he was the only man ever to have fought both Joe Lewis and Jack Dempsey. However, he is most known for his famous and controversial bouts with Max Schmeling and Primo Carnera. He won and lost to both men. He lost on a technical in his final match with Schmeling due to a low blow. It was the only time the title was won on a foul. He was knocked out his second time with Carnera, and many thought the match was rigged, which Sharkey vehemently denied.

Jack was an avid fly-fisherman and great friends with Red Sox great Ted Williams. The two often gave fly-casting demonstrations at the old Boston Sportsman Show. He was said to have been a regular every spring at the bridge in Alton during the salmon run.

Jack retired to Epping, where he was buried in Prospect Cemetery. He died at the age of ninety-one. For many years, he was the oldest living heavyweight champion, only to be beaten again by Max Schmeling, who died at ninety-nine.

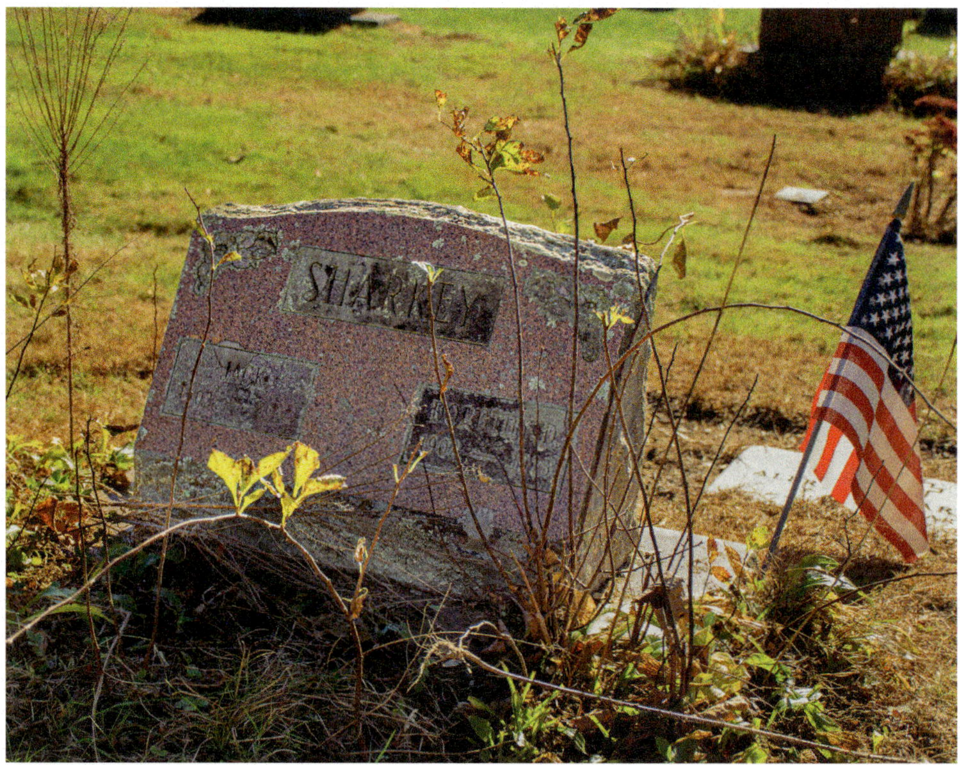

Grave of Jack Sharkey.

4

ODD AND UNUSUAL

Wallace Horse Cemetery, Littleton, NH

Maud, Molly, and Maggie are buried in a small cemetery in Littleton surrounded by a fence. Who are these three ladies? They are horses. After wondering about this burial ground for several years, my wife and I finally stopped by to look. It is intriguing and endearing that someone would love these animals enough to inter them with memorial stones long before construction machinery. Digging a hole in the Granite State can be challenging. So, Bill and I stopped by again to take photos for *Buried New Hampshire*. According to a sign on the fence, Eli Wallace's wife's Bay-Morgans were buried in 1919 with their harnesses, bridles, blankets, and feed boxes.

His wife, Myra, would die in 1920. Eli had purchased Maud and Molly for his wife on her twenty-ninth birthday in 1889. The Wallace family had no children, so Eli, Myra, Maud, and Molly were "a family foursome." Maggie was a working horse that was added later. Arrangements were made for perpetual care of the horse cemetery. Over 100 years later, the memorial to beloved horses still stands. Even the old workhorse Maggie earned her place in this hallowed ground. Oddly, in 2011, part of a mysterious human skull was found in the cemetery. Apparently, it didn't take long to solve the mystery. A woman had buried it there. Someone had given the ancient skull of unknown origin to her husband, and she hadn't known what to do with it after her husband died. So, she buried it in the horse cemetery. The old skull notwithstanding, there is something very touching about the Wallace Horse Cemetery in Littleton. It is a testament to a man's love for his wife and their mutual love for their horses.

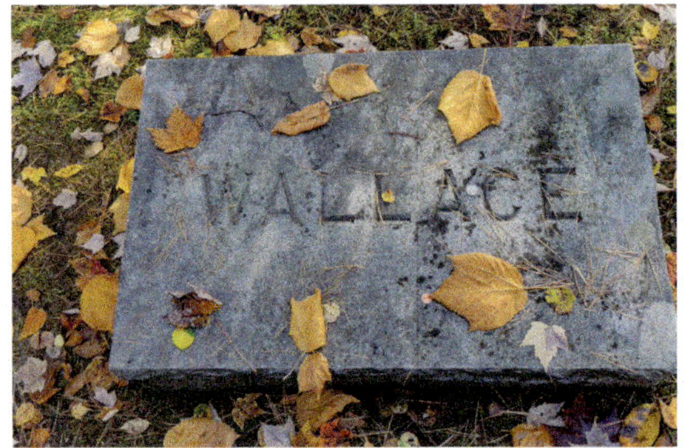

Wallace Horse Cemetery.

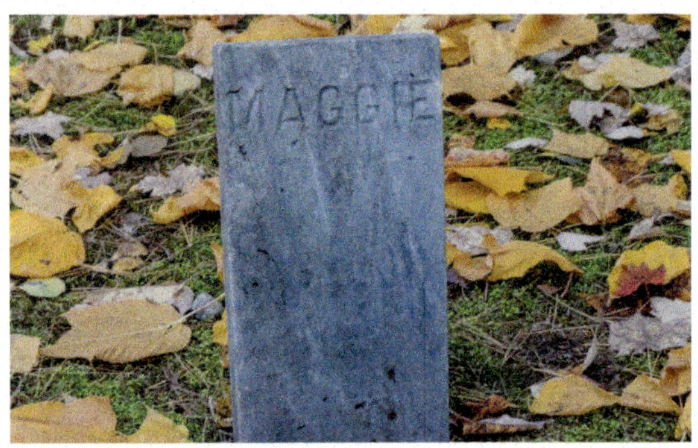

Maggie's stone.

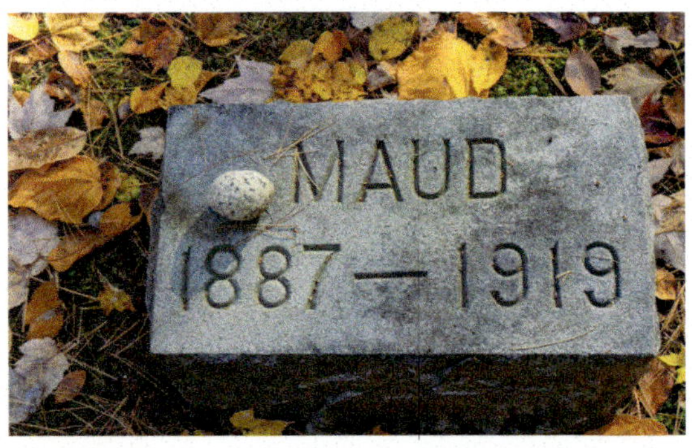

Maud's stone.

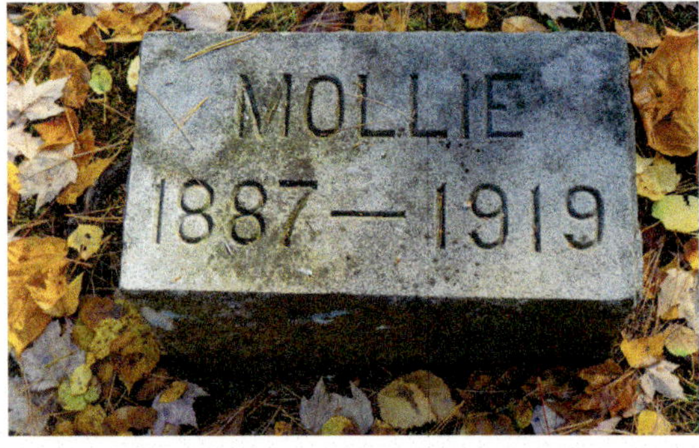

Mollie's stone.

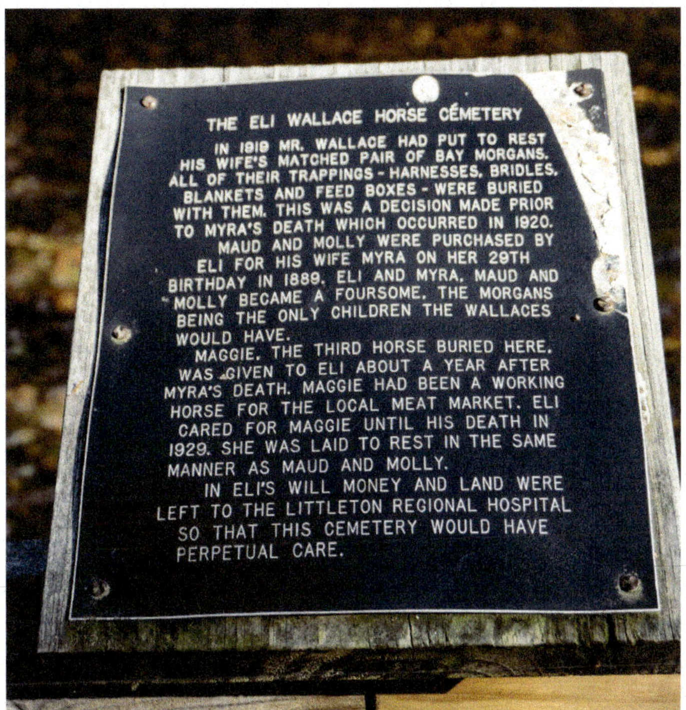

Historical marker at the Wallace Horse Cemetery.

Betty and Barney Hill, "The journey interrupted," Greenwood Cemetery, Kingston

The first well-documented close encounter of the third kind happened in New Hampshire. On the night of September 19, 1961, Betty and Barney were driving home to Portsmouth after a trip to Niagara Falls and Montreal. They were driving on Route 3 when Betty spotted some unusual lights in the sky just south of Lancaster. The lights continued to dog the Hills as they continued their journey through Franconia Notch, past Cannon Mountain, and the Old Man of the Mountain. A mile south of Indian Head, they were allegedly stopped by an alien spaceship and subsequently abducted by extraterrestrials.

The Hills did report the incident to the U.S. Air Force and were interviewed for Operation Blue Book. They did experience some memory loss about the event, and it was suggested that they undergo hypnosis to recall the event. They agreed, and the results were quite amazing; their stories were almost identical. A front-page story in the *Boston Traveler*, based on the tapes of their hypnosis sessions, thrust them into the public eye. In 1966, John Fuller published *The Interrupted Journey*, and they were famous. A made-for-TV movie, *UFO Incident*, followed shortly after. Barney passed away in 1969. Betty continued to tell her story and was a major guest speaker at numerous UFO gatherings. There is a New Hampshire Historical marker in Lincoln, NH, close to where the incident occurred. The dress that Betty was wearing on the night of the abduction, along with hers and Barney's personal papers, are held in the University of New Hampshire's library's historical collection. Both Barney and Betty were very active in the Civil Rights Movement of the 1960s. They were a mixed-race couple, something that was uncommon in those days.

They also had their dog, Delsey, with them. At one point, they stopped the car to walk Delsey and watched the unusual craft that seemed to follow them. There seems to be no reference to where Delsey was at the time of the abduction. The Hills are buried in Greenwood Cemetery in Kingston. The markers are flat to the ground and a little difficult to find. There is some damage to both stones, no doubt the work of souvenir hunters.

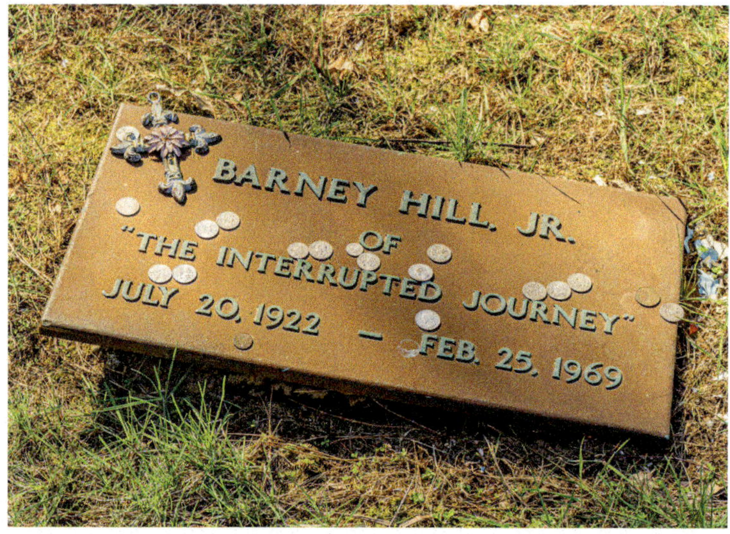

Grave of Barney Hill.

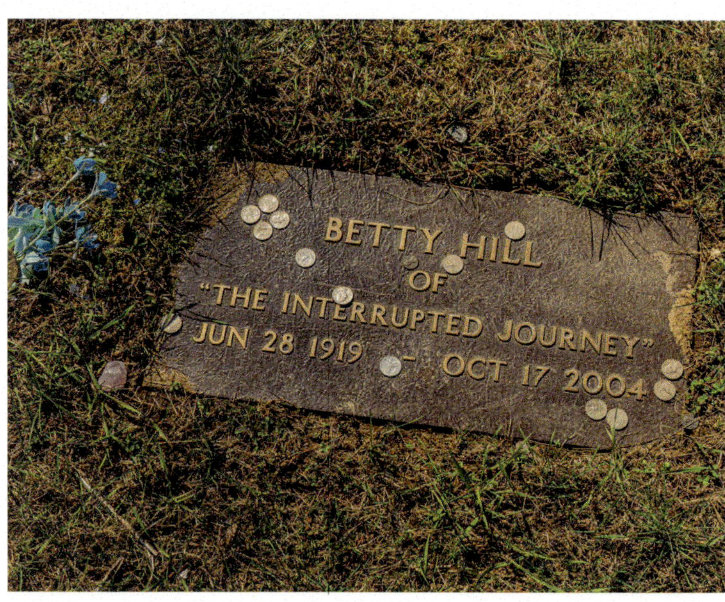

Grave of Betty Hill.

Captain Samuel Jones's Leg, Washington Old Burying Ground

One of the prettiest little towns in New Hampshire is Washington. A beautiful New England Meeting House, built in 1787, sits in the town center next to the *circa* 1840 Congregational Church. Next to both of those landmarks is the Seventh-day Adventist Church, built in 1843, the very first in America. The town is named after George Washington, and its most famous resident is Sylvanus Thayer, the father of the Military Academy (West Point). It was also once the home of Captain Samuel Jones.

What makes Captain Samuel Jones so special? He was the local tavern keeper and an excellent neighbor. In July 1804, Samuel was helping to move the house of a friend when he had an accident in which his leg was crushed. As a result, the leg needed to be amputated.

There was a belief at the time that if an amputated limb was properly buried, the patient would have less pain in the future. The leg was indeed given a funeral complete with a headstone, which can still be viewed today. A slightly more colorful story is that the house movers retired to Samuel's tavern, where they all got roaring drunk to lessen the pain of having a leg removed. At some point during the procedure, they thought it might be a good idea to give the leg a funeral. Either way, Captain Jones's leg lies buried in the old cemetery. It is thought that he moved away to New York or Boston, where the rest of him hopefully is. While you are in the Washington Old Burying Ground, look for the iron headstones; they are unique.

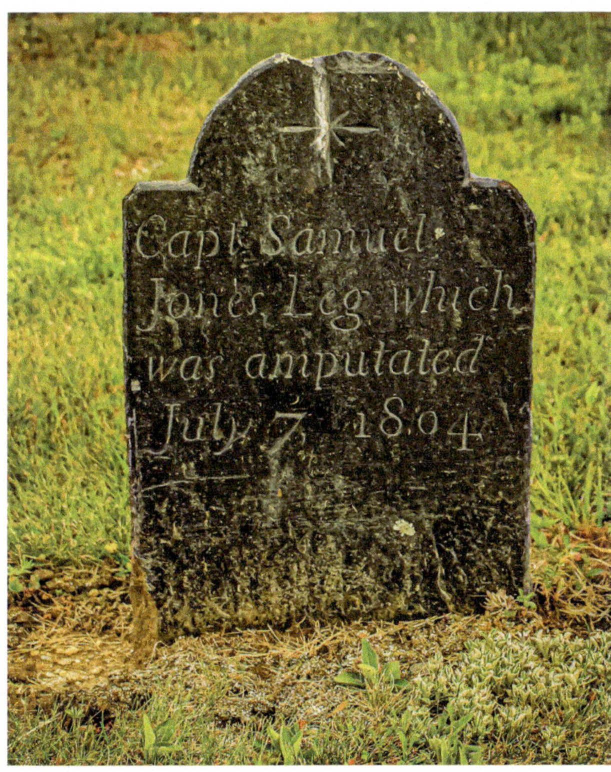

Captain Jones's leg.

The Curious Faces of Abel and Stephen Webster, Chester Village Cemetery, Chester Village

Chester is one of the most picturesque small towns in New Hampshire, and the lovely Village Cemetery is right in the middle of town. The town was established in 1722, and the village center is surrounded by colonial and Federalist Era homes.

In colonial times, most cemeteries were located on the family farm. The first public cemetery in Chester was established in 1751, and some families moved their dead from family plots to the new cemetery in the village. Two former governors of New Hampshire (Samuel and John Bell) and several veterans of the Revolutionary War are buried in the cemetery. The cemetery also has the distinction of having the most signed gravestones, most notably those carved by Stephen and Abel Webster. The two brothers were active stone cutters during the late 1700s, and they are remembered for the odd faces carved on their markers.

The winged death head soul effigy was a common theme on stones of the period. The curious facial expressions set the Websters apart; some effigies are frowning, and others have smiles. There is a great deal of speculation as to why they did this. One theory is that if payment had not been received, then the deceased image was depicted with a frown. If this is true, judging by the number of stones with frowns on them in the Chester cemetery, there were a lot of deadbeats. Another theory is that the brothers expressed their feelings about where the deceased was going to end up in the afterlife. I can only imagine how the family members would feel when they received the finished tombstone and found that dad's marker had a frowning face. Abel Webster is buried in the cemetery, and his brother carved the stone. Apparently, his brother had no idea where he was headed as the stone was adorned with a simple funerary urn. According to New Hampshire author Fritz Wetherbee, Stephen was "Born Again." He was so irked that his Congregational Church would not see the light and convert to the Pentecostal movement, he moved to Hollis.

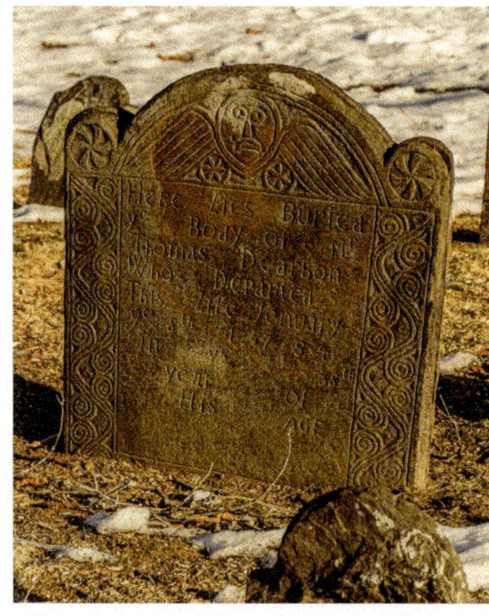

Example of Webster Brothers' stones.

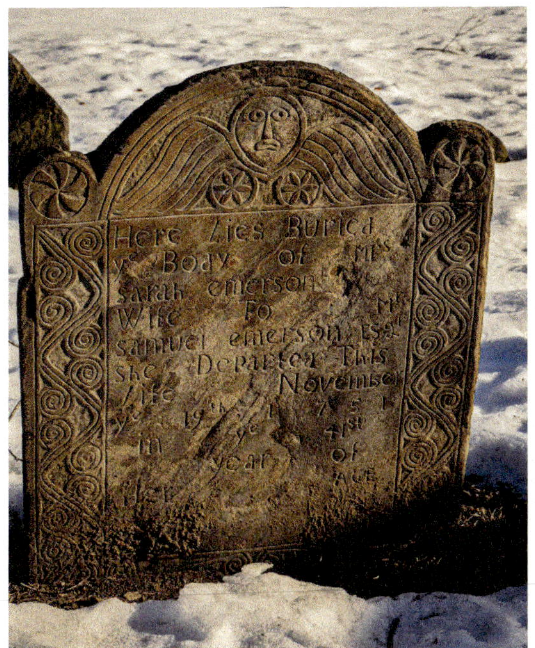

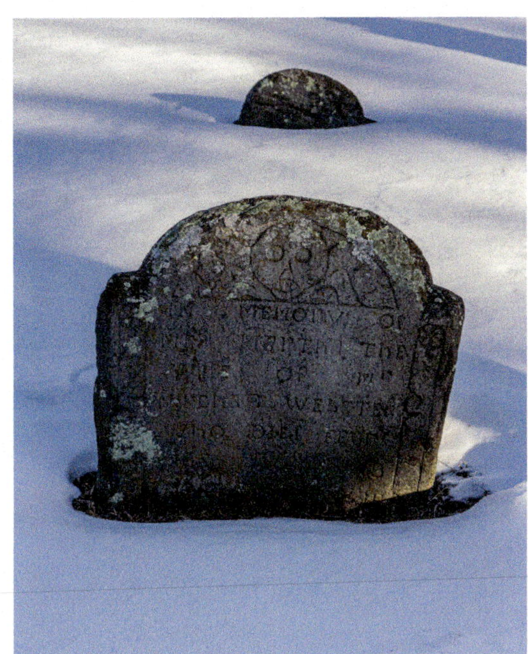

Above left: Example of Webster Brothers' stones.

Above right: Example of Webster Brothers' stones.

Great Stone Chair, The Phillips-Heil Cemetery, Jaffrey

The Phillips-Heil Cemetery in Jaffrey was originally part of a land grant that would include the Phillips-Exeter Academy granted to the wealthy Phillips family from Massachusetts. Lt. Governor Samuel Phillips, a frequent visitor to Jaffrey, sold the land for a nominal fee to Captain Joseph Perkins and Abraham Ross, among others. This was on the condition that a stone wall would surround the burial ground. That wall, not surprisingly, still exists today. One monument stands out when one passes the stone posts leading into the burial ground. It is a great stone chair, fit for a king, that sits in the Ross Family Plot. That family lived in the area for three generations. Three other Rosses are buried here, but the throne belongs to J. Ross. The chair perhaps waits for Mr. Ross's eventual spiritual return to earth. He died in 1871, and after a long journey, he would return to a place where he could rest and enjoy the sunset and a view of Gap Mountain.

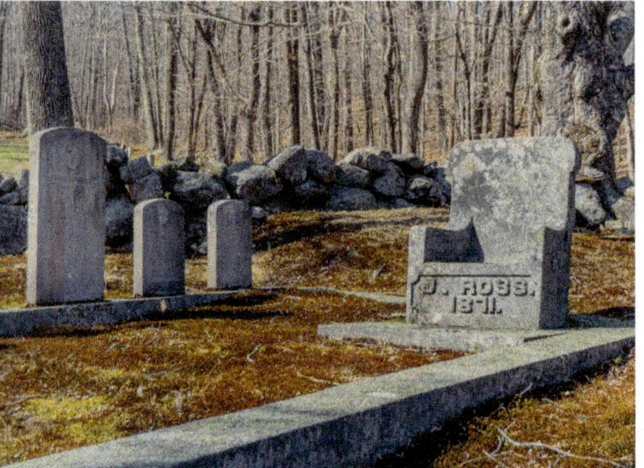

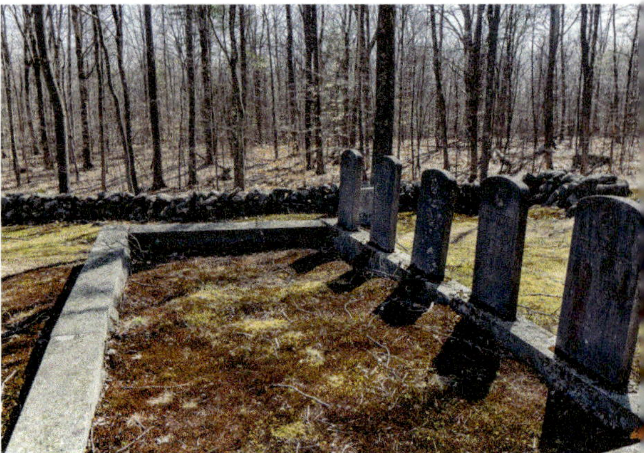

Above left: The Great Chair in Jaffery.

Above right: The graves next to the Great Chair.

Fido Maloon, A Faithfull Dog, Meeting Huse Cemetery, Meredith

In the picturesque Meeting House Cemetery on Meredith Neck are buried the remains of the Maloon family, including their faithful and much-loved dog, Fido. The small stone reads:

FIDO.
"He mourneth the loss of his master"
AE. 15 yrs

His owner was David Maloon, who died in 1879. Fido passed a short time later and is buried close by his master. A fitting place for a good dog.

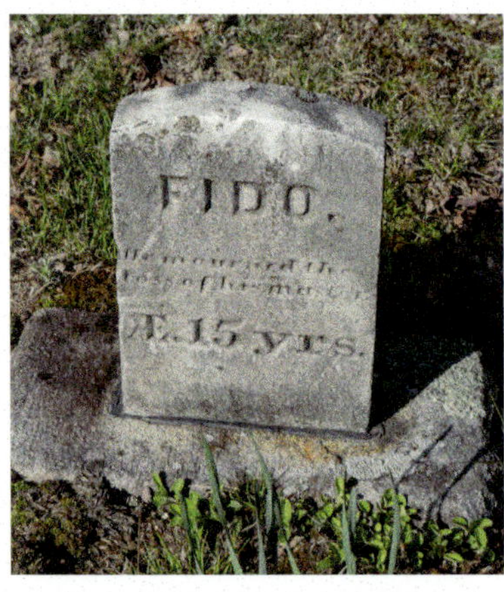

Fido's grave, the family dog.

Emil A. Hanslin (1920–1987), Loaf of Bread Grave, Old Main Street Cemetery, New London

"With Breadth and Depth, He Cared" is inscribed on Emil Hanslin's unique gravestone. His memorial looks like a large loaf of bread. Mr. Hanslin was not a baker but a builder. He received awards for his communities, Eastman near Grantham and New Seabury on Cape Cod. His father was a builder, so Hanslin grew up "swinging a hammer," but the theater was his first love. He studied drama at the University of Arizona and taught theater in Boston until World War II when he joined the Army Air Corps. After the war, he became a developer and a builder after working briefly as a theater director. He developed and marketed Post and Beam Yankee Barn Homes. His homes were featured in numerous magazines, including *Life*. Yankee Barn Homes is still in business under new ownership.

Bill and I initially thought that Mr. Hanslin must have been a baker. After reading his obituary, I suspect the memorial was not designed with bread in mind. Be that as it may, the talented Emil A. Hanslin attracts attention for his innovations in home building and his unique crypt, which looks, indeed, like a giant loaf of bread.

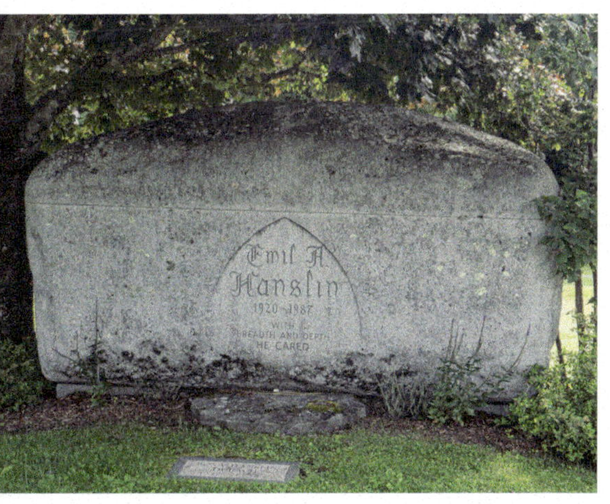

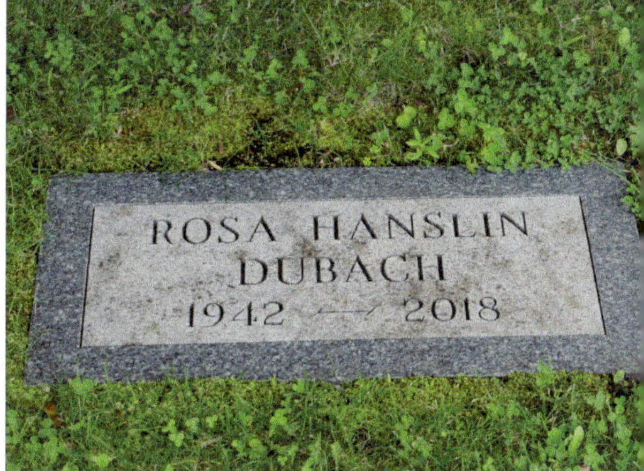

Above left: Emil Hanslin's crypt.

Above right: Emil Hanslin's wife.

Smallpox Cemetery, Jaffrey

Smallpox epidemics were commonplace in New England in the seventeenth and eighteenth centuries. Today, thanks to inoculation, smallpox is a thing of the past. Oddly, they knew the science of vaccination but were reluctant to undergo the procedure. Sounds a lot like today. One of New England's earliest documentations of the smallpox plague was in Boston in 1721. Cotton Mather had heard of the procedure from his servant and slave Onesimus, who had seen it done in West Africa, where he had been born. Mather asked Doctor Zabdiel Boylston to give it a try. Both men were severely criticized by the locals and clergy for their efforts. The clergy argued that smallpox was the will of God and his way of punishing sinful people. So much was the opposition that Boylston had to go into hiding, and Mather and Boylston had their homes firebombed. For the record, Boylston vaccinated enough people to prove it worked.

In another disease outbreak in 1764, people were less reluctant to have the procedure done. The governor of Massachusetts organized a group of doctors to give vaccinations for free. One of those doctors was Joseph Warren, the man who sent Paul Revere on his famous ride and died on Bunker Hill. George Washington is credited with saving the American Revolution by ordering his soldiers to be vaccinated.

Smallpox remained a major cause of death in New England long after the Revolution. Jaffrey is not the only town in New Hampshire to have a smallpox cemetery. Some are known, but many more have been lost to time. Jaffrey is unique in that, in 1985, the town placed a memorial stone at the location. The outbreak happened in 1792, and none of the graves had been marked. The large granite boulder records the names of the six interned in the cemetery. Two of whom were Revolutionary War veterans, and Nancy Thorndike, who died at the age of twelve.

The cemetery is on private land, although there is public access. The path is marked and requires about a ten-minute walk to reach the cemetery.

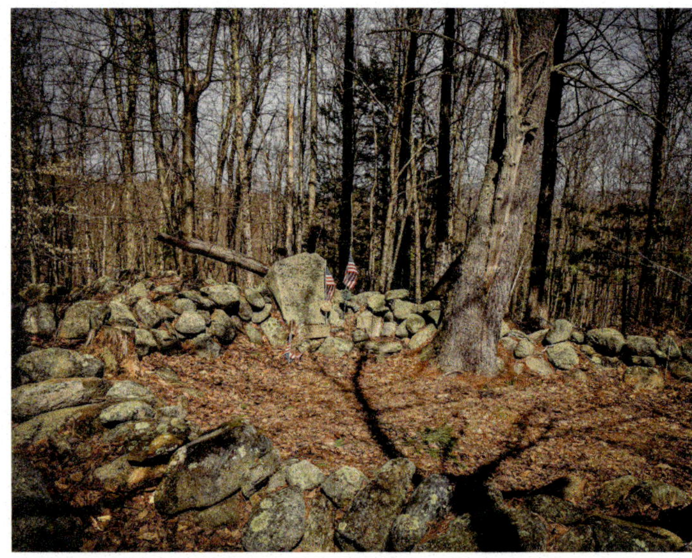

Smallpox Cemetery in Jaffery.

Dorothy Caldwell (1869–1926), The Old Burying Ground, Jaffrey

The tomb of Dorothy Caldwell is a love story set in stone. In a nutshell, a beautiful young American girl goes to Paris, meets a young artist, and they fall in love. The couple has a daughter who dies in infancy. The mother dies shortly after, but not before expressing her desire to be buried in a place she loved as a child. Dorothy Caldwell was that girl, and artist and sculpturer Viggo Brandt-Erichsen was the young man.

Dorothy had summered in Jaffrey while growing up and had many fond memories of the town and the surrounding natural beauty. She asked to be buried in the shadow of Mount Monadnock. After her death, Viggo had her and their daughter's remains cremated and carried them to Jaffrey, where they were entombed in the Old Burying Ground. Viggo spent two years living at the Ark, a local hotel, constructing the mausoleum and sculpturing the face of his beloved wife for her final resting place.

Viggo spent many years living in Jaffrey, where he was a much-loved and respected community member. He remarried twice, the second with the same outcome as the first; she died shortly after their marriage. The third time was to an artist named Martha Mott. While in Jaffrey, he created the moving sculpture *The Buddies* for the town's monument to those who served and died in World War I. In 1948, he and Martha moved to California, where they died in 1955.

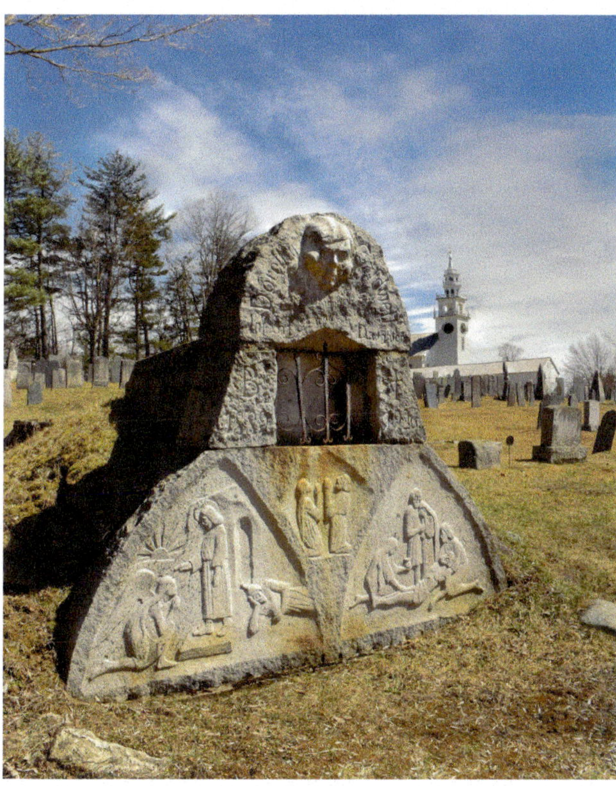

Grave of Dorothy Caldwell.

5
HAUNTED

Gilson Road Cemetery, Nashua

Gilson Road Cemetery is one of New Hampshire's most notorious haunted locations. Judging by the internet, the little burial ground is the state's number one destination for paranormal investigators. It is safe to say that Gilson Road Cemetery has gained national urban legend status. There are stories of the cemetery having been the site of a fierce battle between Native American tribes and a mysterious medicine man. The area is known for an unexplained fog that envelops the cemetery. There is, of course, a lady in white, the specters of children, and the sound of children laughing. There may be some credence to this story as there are quite a few graves of children in the cemetery. People who visit the cemetery often leave small toys and candy on their graves. Odd lights and orbs appear in countless photographs of the place, but none appear in any of Rick's or mine. There is also the ghostly motorcyclist, known as the Watcher, who roars by only to disappear.

Not much is known of the cemetery's origin; the earliest marked grave dates to 1796. It obviously became the family burial ground of the Gilson family. The gravestone of John Gilson is dated 1811. There are numerous graves of the Gilson children, most notably that of young Walter Gilson, who died at the age of five. What is peculiar about Walter's stone is the perfect round hole drilled through the center. There are many theories as to why; however, there is no logical explanation. The creepiest story of all is that of Betty Gilson. If you stand at the gate and yell: "Betty, I have your baby," she will appear. Who can blame her?

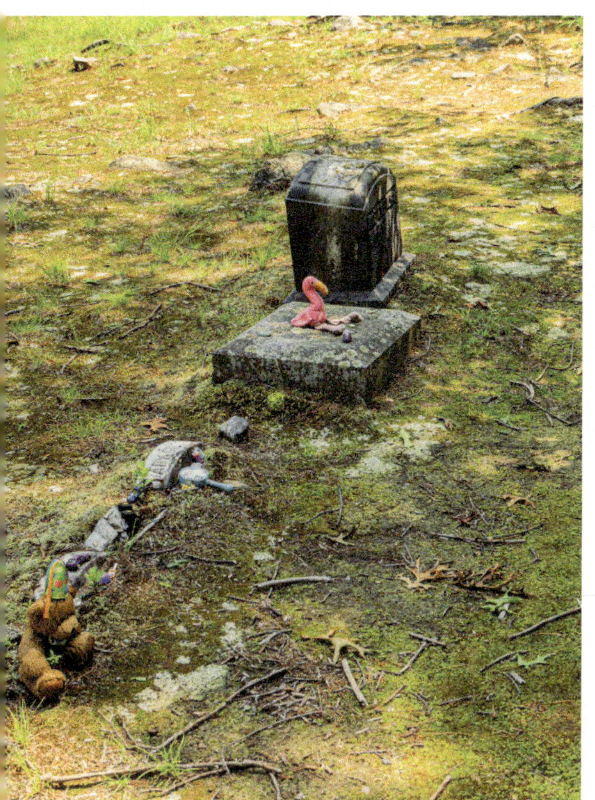

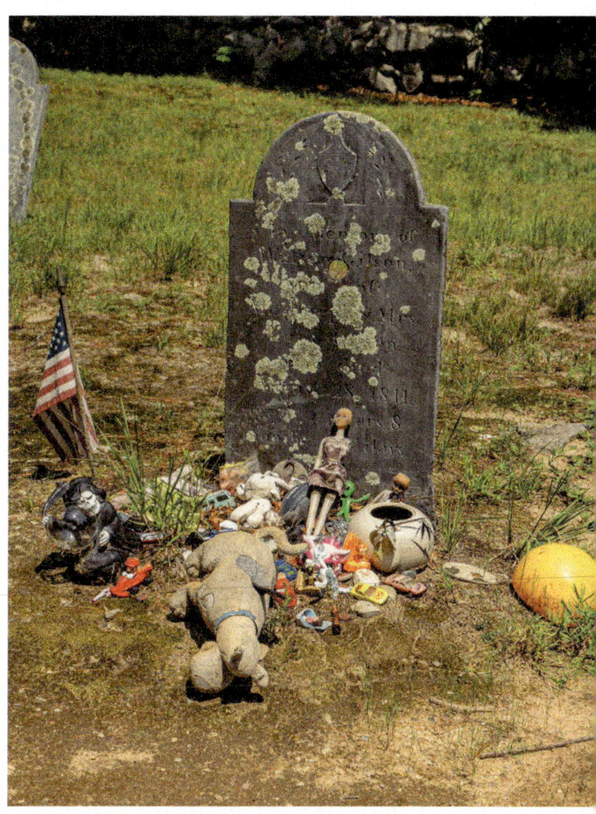

Above left: Gilson children.

Above right: Walter Gilson.

Right: Gilson Cemetery gate.

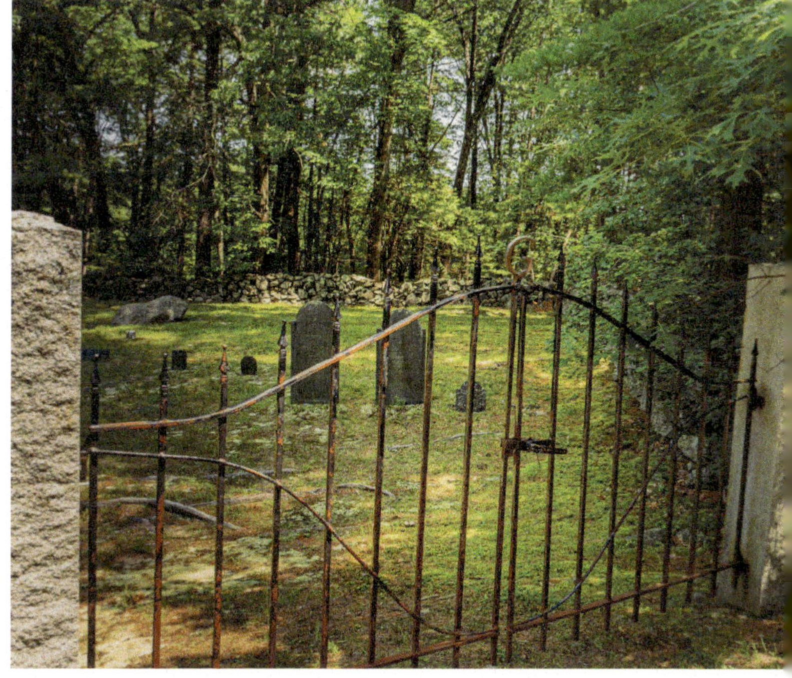

The Mysterious Glowing Stone of Portsmouth's South Cemetery

While Rick and I were visiting the Portsmouth Athenaeum doing some research on the South Cemetery, I came across an article by George Hoster from the *Portsmouth Herald* newspaper. The article told of a curious gravestone in South Cemetery that glowed. Apparently, the stone gives off a luminous glow in all kinds of weather and was a well-known attraction for local college students and would-be ghost hunters. Local author Roxie J. Zwicker mentions the stone or stones in her book *New Hampshire Book of the Dead.* Zwicker reports that more than one stone glows and that a black figure sometimes appears behind the stones. It is also said that cameras sometimes malfunction when in the vicinity.

Of course, Rick and I were intrigued and began looking for more information. I mentioned the story to Cynthia Mulcahy, who had previously helped us locate other graves in South Cemetery. She had not heard the story but was immediately on the case. A few days later, she reported that she had found the grave. We arranged to meet, and I was fortunate enough to spend a couple of hours one afternoon exploring South Cemetery with Cynitha and photographing the mysterious glowing stone. At this point, we had no idea if the story was true. However, she vowed to return with some of her friends after dark. Her first attempt proved fruitless, as it was early evening, and biting bugs forced an early retreat. A second, more organized attempt was met with disappointment as the stone failed to glow. I cannot speak for those who claim to have seen the glow, but I trust Cynitha and am sticking with her story.

On the other hand, on the day that I visited the site with Cynitha, the SD card in my camera malfunctioned. I clearly remember checking the images I took of the stone, but I only rechecked the camera once I got home. When I placed the card on my computer, it was empty. A couple of weeks later, accompanied by my son. I reshot the images, this time with no ill effects. I have used this same card numerous times since that day with no problems.

As we have said elsewhere in these pages, neither Rick nor I are ghost hunters. However, we do keep an open mind.

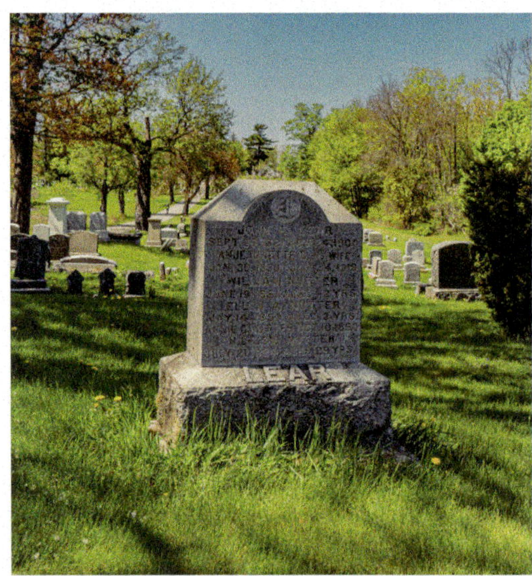

Glowing stone.

6

WHITE MOUNTAINS

Ethan Allen and Lucy Crawford, Crawford Cemetery, Carroll

It would be impossible to write the history of the White Mountains of New Hampshire without including Ethan Allen Crawford and his wife, Lucy. Born to Abel and Hannah Crawford in 1792, one of nine children. He grew up in what was then known as White Mountain Notch, roaming the hills with his father, hunting, and fishing. He was quite large in stature and rugged. He was known as the "Giant of the Notch." In 1811, he left the Notch to join the army and served in the War of 1812. He worked for a time in New York and had intended to settle there. However, at the request of his grandfather, Eleazar Rosebrook, he was persuaded to return to the Notch. Eleazar was in ill health and could not run his tavern at Giant's Grave. In return for his help, he was promised the property upon the death of Eleazar. Ethan did inherit the inn along with the mortgage. At the same time, Ethan married his cousin Lucy Hall, Eleazar's granddaughter. In 1818, Ethan returned from a trip to find his inn in flames and his wife lying in a bed outside, having just given birth to their child. The inn was remortgaged and rebuilt. Ethan and his father were in continuous debt; Ethan served a jail sentence because of his indebtedness. Despite these setbacks, Ethan's accomplishments were legendary. He created the first path to the top of Mount Washington with his father. He also constructed a bridle path to the summit. In his seventies, Abel was the first man to ride to the top of Mount Washington on a horse. He built three stone huts on Washington to accommodate hikers. He guided many of the day's most important authors, painters, and political figures, including National Hawthorne, Henry David Thoreau, Ralph Waldo Emerson, and Daniel Webster. He is credited with guiding the first party of women to ascend the mountain. In 1820, Ethan guided the Weeks-Bracket Party, which named most of the peaks in the Presidential Range. The Weeks Act, which created the National Forest system, is named for James Wingate Weeks. Ethan also served two terms in the New Hampshire House. He died in 1869. The inscription on his headstone reads:

He built here the first Hotel at the White Mountains, of which he was the owner and landlord for many years. He was of great native talent & sagacity, of noble, kind & benevolent disposition, a beloved husband and father, and an honest & good man.

Lucy Crawford

It is said that there is an even greater woman behind every great man, and Lucy Crawford was just that. There is conflicting information on how many children the Crawfords had; some say five sons, and another source says there were at least three sons and a daughter. As one author commented: "in the privations of the White Mountains." As previously stated, her first child was born outside of her home while it was in flames. She was also a vital part of managing the tavern. She made her first climb to the top of Mount Washington in 1825. However, she is remembered today for writing the first history of the White Mountains. Her 1846 book *History of the White Mountains* is still in print today.

Ethan and Lucy are buried in a family cemetery near the Cog Railroad in Carroll, New Hampshire. Their mutual grandfather, Captain Eleazar Rosebrook, is buried in the same plot. Ironically, condominiums surround the little cemetery. One must wonder what Lucy and Ethan would have thought.

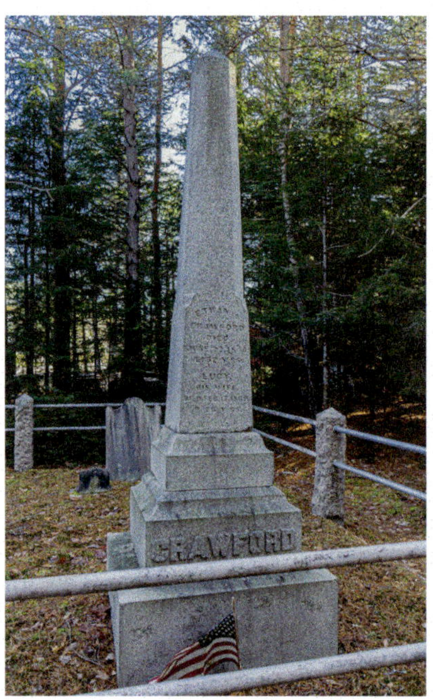

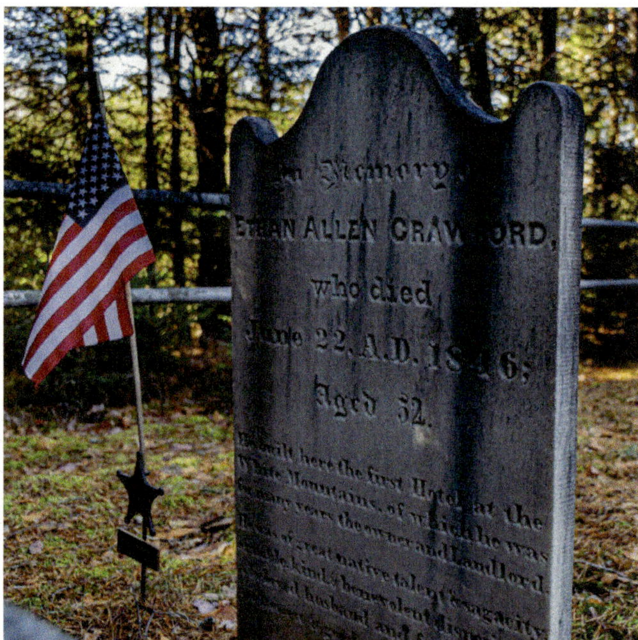

Above left: Ethan and Lucy Crawford.

Above right: Ethan Crawford's marker.

English Jack (1824–1912), "The Hermit of Crawford Notch," Straw Cemetery, Carroll

One of the more endearing stories of the White Mountains is that of John Alfred Vials, also known as "English Jack" or "Jack the Hermit." Jack lived in a rude shack not far from the railroad tracks at the head of Crawford Notch. He came to the Notch to work on the Portland and Ogdensburg Railroad in 1875. Born in 1824, he was then orphaned and lived in poverty in London. He became a sailor, was shipwrecked, survived on a desert island, and was eventually rescued and returned to London. Upon his return to London, he discovered that the woman he intended to marry had died. He then joined the Royal Navy, served in the Crimean War, and eventually wound up in New Hampshire.

Jack was not your typical hermit; he advertised himself by placing signs near the Notch railroad station directing visitors to his cabin. He sold homemade beer, souvenir canes that he made, and postcards of himself in front of his home. He made a good living. He entertained his visitors by telling his tale and sometimes eating frogs and snakes. Over the years, he was visited by hundreds of travelers visiting the Notch. Many notable people of their day made the trek to see the "Hermit of the Notch." You might say that he was the founder of the first tourist trap in the "Whites." Jack lived year-round in his cabin for most of the years he resided in the Notch. In the last years of his life, he did winter with a couple of families who lived in Twin Mountain. He died in 1912 while staying with the McGee family in Twin Mountain. His obituary was published in *The New York Times*:

> You see me here, a hermit, old and gray
> And bearing hard on three-score years and ten
> Like others you have wondered, I dare say
> What brought me here, away from haunts of men.

A verse from *The Story of Jack, The Hermit of the White Mountains*
James E. Mitchell, 1891

Jack is buried in Straw Cemetery in Carroll. The cemetery is located beside busy Route 3 and is easy to find.

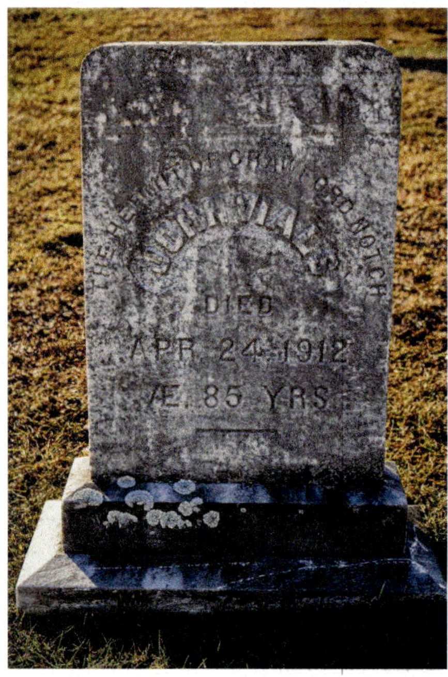

Grave of John Vials.

The Willey Family Cemetery, Tragedy in the White Mountains, North Conway

In August 1826, a violent thunderstorm swept through Crawford Notch, causing the Saco River to flood and a terrible landslide that swept away the entire Willey family. It had been a sweltering summer that had made the earth extremely dry and unstable. Samuel Willey Jr. had opened an inn halfway between Abel Crawford's Inn in Hart's Location and Ethan Crawford's at Fabyan a year before the disaster. The new inn proved to be much needed and quite successful. Sam had moved from Conway to the location with his wife, Polly, and five children: four girls, a son, and another boy they had taken in. A hired hand was also living under the same roof. A couple of smaller storms and a more minor landslide had given an early warning as to what might happen. Sam had made some preparations by building a rough shelter outside the home in case of a landslide. The storm began in the afternoon of the 28th and lasted throughout the night. Sometime during the night, the towering cliff behind their home gave way. No one knows exactly what happened; however, at some point, the family left the warmth of their home, perhaps to seek the safety of the shelter. What is known is that the following day, when Ethan Crawford and another man arrived at the house, the family was nowhere to be found. Amazingly, the house had been spared and was intact. The home's interior was in disarray, and the family bible was open to the Nineteenth Psalm: "The heavens declare the glory of God and the firmament showeth His handiwork." A large boulder behind the house had split the landslide, and it passed on either side of the structure. Others arrived from Conway, and a search was organized. The first to be found was the hired hand and then Polly, who was nearby. Later, Sam was found in a brook. Three children were found on the second day of the search. The other three were never found.

The news of the tragedy caused a sensation in the newspapers of the day, and it was not long before the home became a tourist destination. Many painters and authors visited the site. Nathaniel Hawthorne wrote a short story about the incident called "The Ambitious Guest." Although the house no longer exists, the State of New Hampshire has an interpretive area at the site. It is an excellent place to stop and buy an ice cream while contemplating what was.

The Willey family are buried in a small family cemetery in North Conway, located on private property. The location is somewhat obscure, although it is not more than 100 yards off Route 16. If you have ever traveled along this stretch on a busy weekend, you might have waited in traffic right next to it and not have known it was there. It is behind one of the most popular restaurants in the town. The phrase, "isn't that enough to give you the willies?" is said to come from the story.

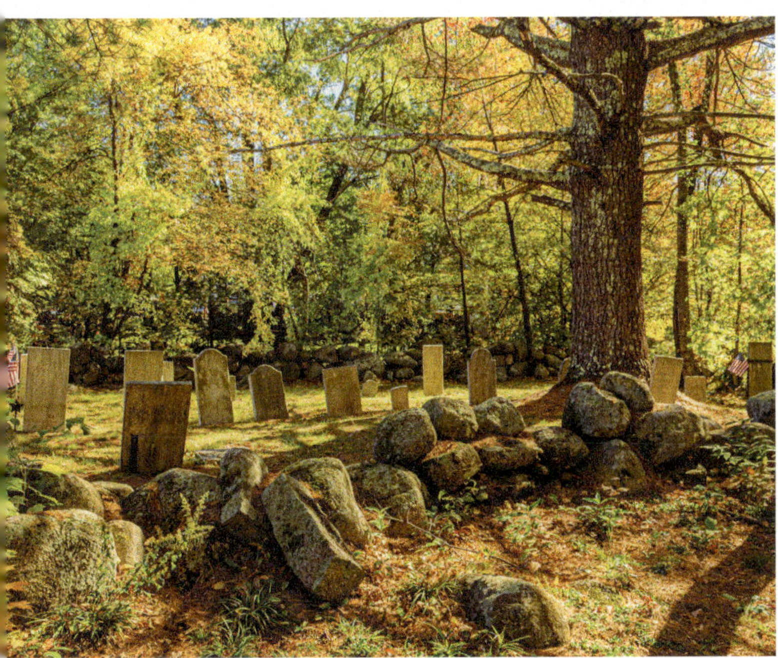

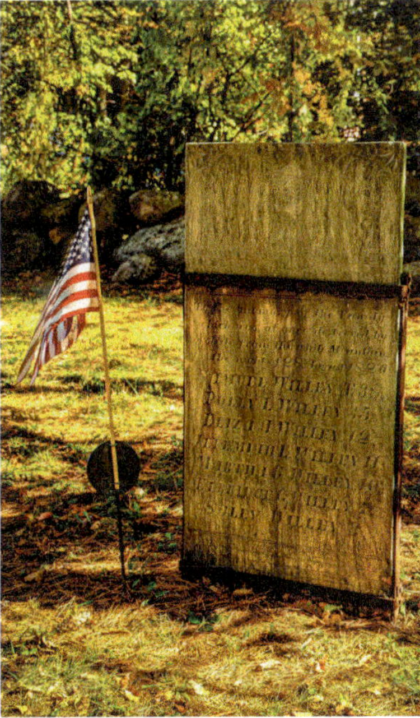

Above left: View of the Willey family cemetery.

Above right: The Willey marker.

7

VETERANS (THOSE WHO SERVED)

Old Tom (died 1885), at Riverside Cemetery, Alton

If you go to the Riverside Cemetery in Alton, you can't miss Old Tom's grave. It sits inside a white picket fence. Old Tom isn't a wealthy deceased citizen. He is a horse. A horse that, along with his owner, Major John Savage, survived, not unscathed, the battle of Chancellorsville during the Civil War. Both were welcomed back to Alton as heroes. Major Savage claimed Old Tom had saved his life. Savage felt so loyal to his horse that he asked the powers in the town that when the time came, Old Tom be buried in the Riverside Cemetery near his own grave site. This turned out to be a controversial request. On the one hand, Old Tom and his owner were highly regarded veterans; on the other hand, if the town allowed a horse to be buried in the town cemetery, everyone would want to bury their pets there. A compromise was reached. It was agreed that Old Tom could be buried outside the graveyard near the Major's grave.

Major George Savage died in 1883, Old Tom died in 1885, and the town honored the compromise that had been reached. Old Tom was buried just outside the cemetery border, near his master's final resting place. Of course, things change over time. Many more people have been laid to rest in the Riverside Cemetery. The original graveyard fence has been moved to allow for expansion, and now Old Tom lies in the center of the cemetery. Major Savage would probably approve. Apparently, an unknown benefactor took care of the upkeep of old Tom's Grave for many years.

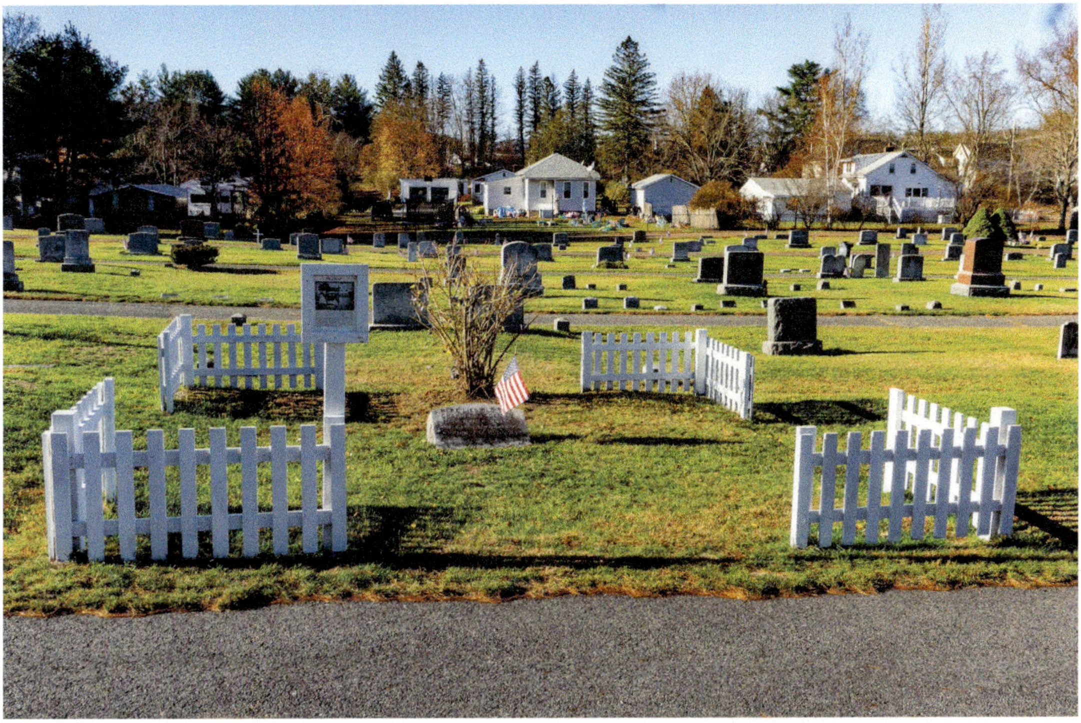

Above: Old Tom Riverside Cemetery, Alton.

Right: Savage family plot, including Major John Savage.

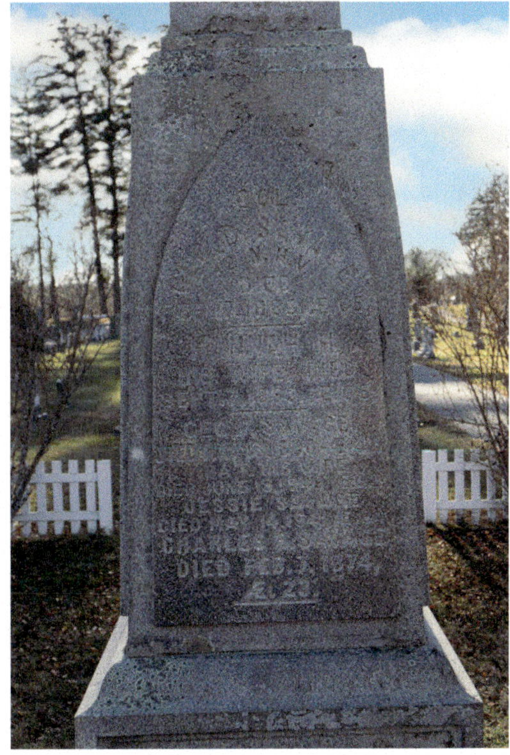

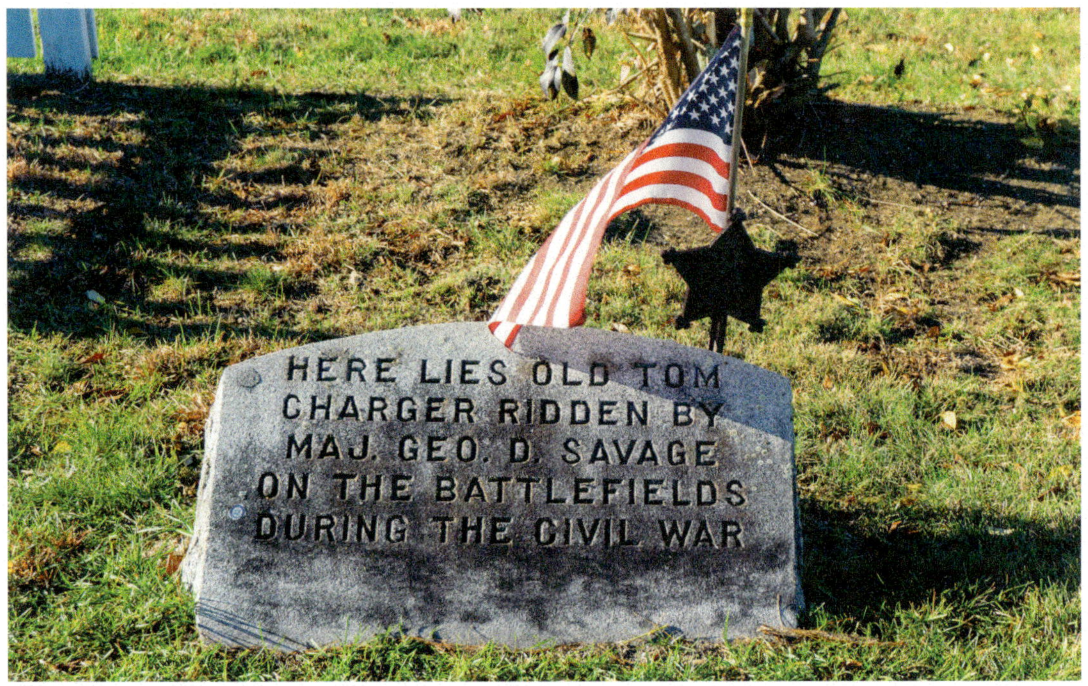

Above: Old Tom's marker.

Left: Old Tom's Historical marker.

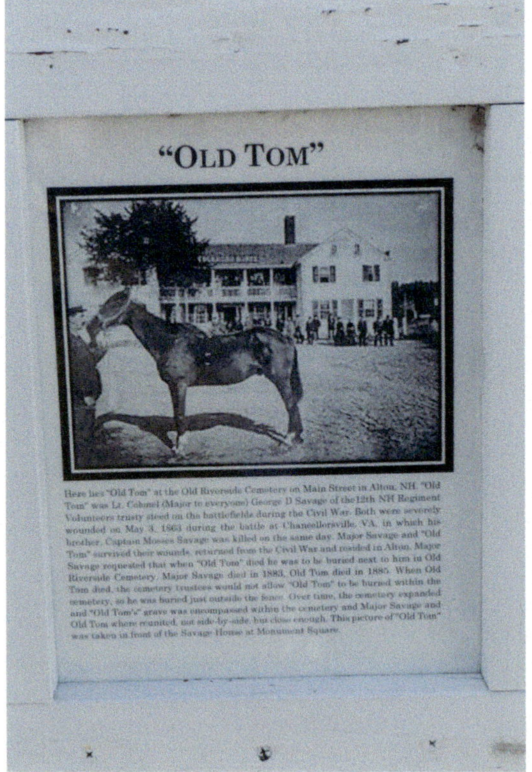

8
MURDER MOST FOUL

Anethe Matea (1847–1873) and Karen Christensen (1833–1873), South Cemetery, Portsmouth

On March 5, 1873, Louis Wagner, a trusted handyman and friend of the Norwegian Hontvet family who lived on the Isles of Shoals, rowed 6 miles to steal $600 from the family who had previously kindly taken him in. That night, only three women were in the house on Smuttynose Island, Maine. All the men and fishermen were in Portsmouth waiting for a bait delivery. Wagner figured it would be easy to steal the money, but it didn't turn out that way. Instead, it turned into "the crime of the century."

Using an ax, Wagner murdered Anethe Matea and Karen Christensen. Maren Hontvet escaped. The story is too complicated and controversial to tell here. Anethe and Karen are buried in South Cemetery in Portsmouth. *A Memorable Murder* by well-known Isle of Shoals poet Celia Thaxter tells the story vividly from the point of view of having known everyone involved. The story was initially published in the *Atlantic* magazine. In Celia's eyes, innocent, happy lives were interrupted by a horrifying evil. *Mystery on the Isles of Shoals: Closing the Case on the Smuttynose Ax Murders of 1873* by J. Dennis Robinson convincingly provides evidence to substantiate charismatic Louis Wagner's guilt while dispelling Wagner's desperate accusation of Maren's guilt. Novelist Anita Shreve's fictional novel *The Weight of Water* and the film of the same name did much to advance Maren's guilt theory. Wagner also accused several other unlikely suspects.

Some doubted that anyone could row the distance in eleven hours. During a reenactment, a seventy-five-year-old businessman rowed the same route in two hours and fourteen minutes in a replica wooden boat. There is plenty to read about relative to this vicious murder. Make up your own mind. Two young women's lives were grievously cut short. Bill and I were not having much luck finding Anethe's and Karen's tombstones when we approached two women out for a walk and inquired as to the location of the graves. They weren't sure, so we moved on. A few minutes later, we noticed four arms waving in the air. The two ladies had found Anethe's and Karen's resting place. One also took out a phone and called a relative, one of the cemetery owners. He showed us where John W. Parsons, MD (1841–1912), the doctor who performed the autopsy on Anethe and Karen, is buried. Thank you to both ladies for taking time from their walk on a beautiful day to help two lost photographers.

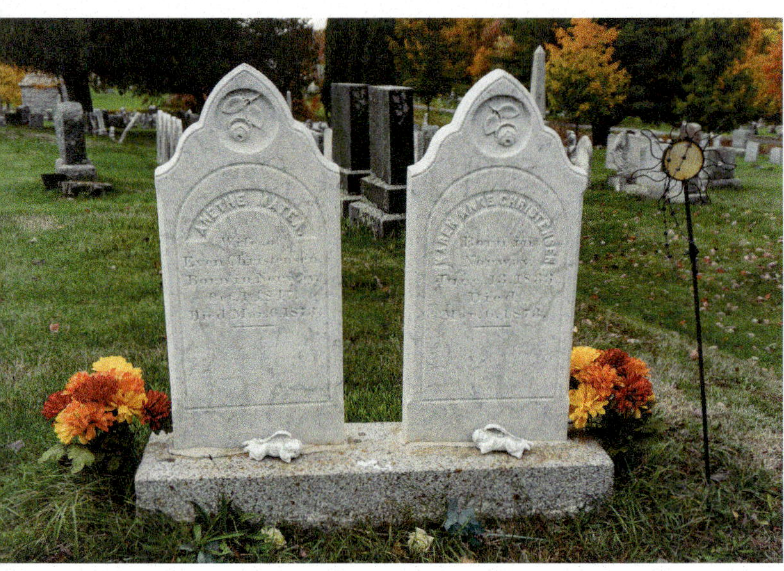

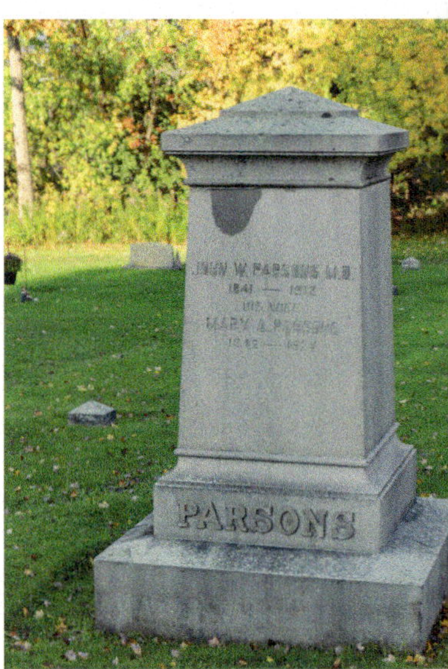

Above right: Anethe Matea and Karen Christensen.

Above left: Dr. John Parsons conducted an autopsy on the Smuttynose victims.

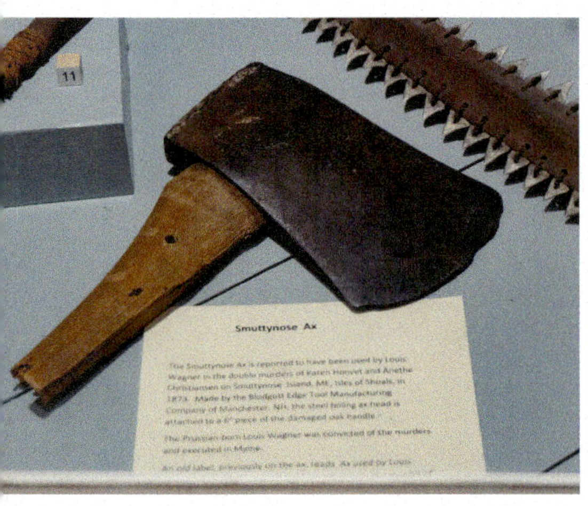

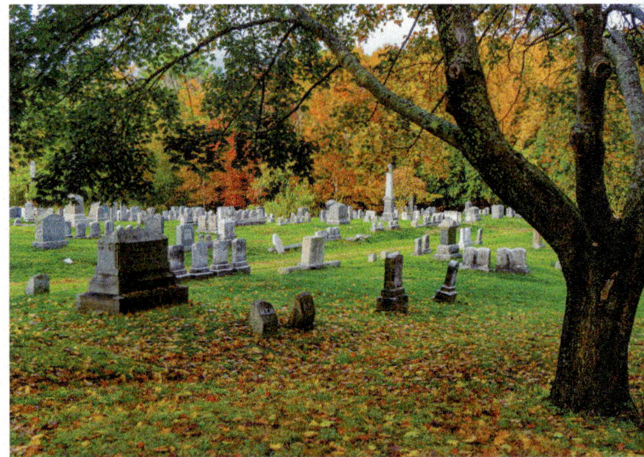

Above right: Murder weapon. (*Portsmouth Athenaeum*)

Above left: South Cemetery.

Sally Cochran (1805–1833), Old North Pembroke Cemetery, Pembroke

Bill and I visited the Pembroke Library to research the notorious 1875 murder of Josie Langmaid. While perusing copies of old newspapers, I discovered that there had been a murder of another young girl in Pembroke. This one pre-dated Josie Langmaid's. Twenty-eight-old Sally Cochran was beaten to death with a fence post by a trusted farm hand in 1833. Josie was not alone in having her life cut short similarly in this quintessential small New Hampshire town. Josie has an obelisk commemorating the spot where she was murdered. A stone inscribed with 1833 is in a remote field not far away from Josie's memorial, marking where Sally died. The story as it appeared in newsprint and legal documents appeared to be a simple one.

Sally lived on a farm with her husband, Chauncey, and an eighteen-year-old farmhand, Abraham Prescott. The farmhand had worked for the family since he was fifteen. One Sunday in June, Sally and Abraham walked to a nearby field to pick wild strawberries. Abraham killed Sally. Chancey, who had stayed at home, heard Abraham in the barn where he, in tears, admitted to the murder by telling his employer that he had "struck Mrs. Cochran with a stake." Had Abraham and Sally had a relationship? Had Sally rebuked the young man's advances? Chancey testified that he fully trusted his wife. Perhaps the farm hand was trying to eliminate his employers so that he could take ownership of the property. Abraham claimed that he had been asleep when he attacked the young girl. Oddly enough, the trusted young man had, while sleepwalking, attacked Sally and Chauncey with the butt end of an ax while they were sleeping six months earlier. Although both the man and wife were injured, they forgave the farmhand. It took two trials to convict Abraham even though he had confessed to the murder. Some jurors talked in public about the first trial. This led to a mistrial. A verse account of the confession suggests one motive: "Oh! lust, accursed lust! 'twas this for which I did the deed; Forfeiting heaven, and life, and bliss, Forfeiting all I need."

Another, presented by the defense, was a form of mental illness, somnambulism. How often was mental illness used as a defense in those days? How well would such a defense work for a lower-class laborer? It didn't. Abraham Prescott was hanged on January 6, 1836. The town raised the money to have the convicted murderer buried in Rumney. This was to prevent the body from being donated for medical research. For further insight into this story, check out Leslie Rounds' recently published book *I Have Struck Mrs. Cochran with a Stake*. Leslie Lambert Rounds is the executive director of Maine's Saco Museum. She discovered an unfinished piece of embroidery that captured her imagination. According to Rounds, in a Seacoast Online column by J. Dennis Robinson, the needlepoint embroidery features a flowery border around a tombstone with the names and dates of birth of nine Cochran children. It appeared that death dates would be added later. At the bottom of the sampler, "wrought by Sally Cochran in 1818," is the verse: "Each moment has its sickle and cuts down / The fairest bloom of sublunary bliss."

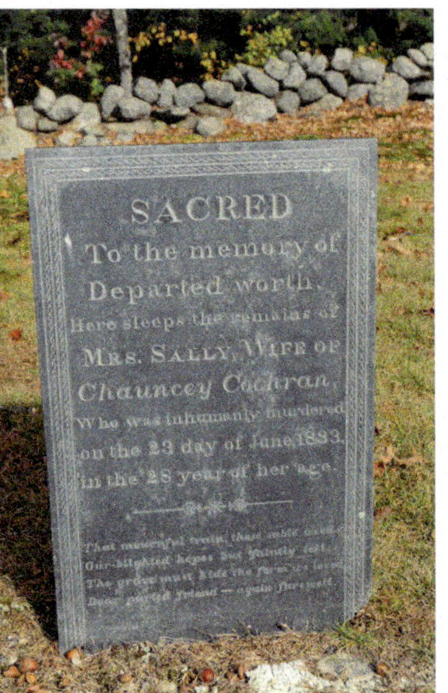

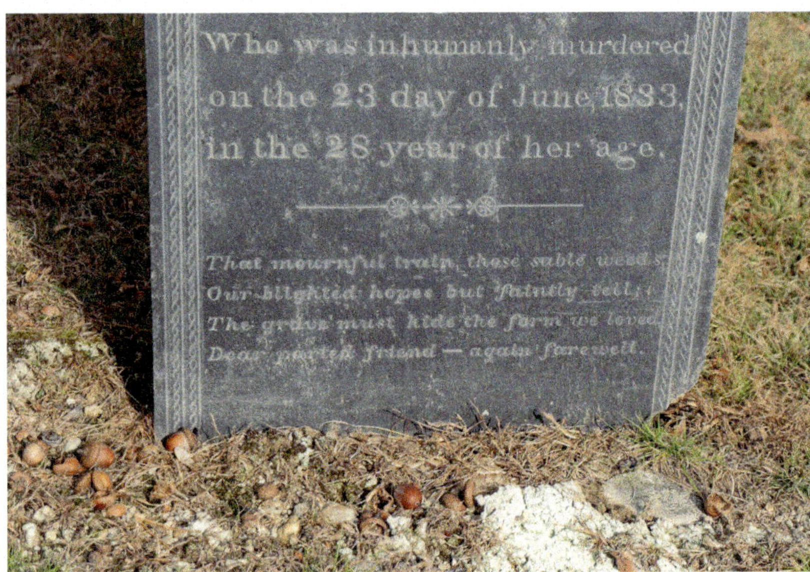

Above left: Grave of Sally Cochran.

Above right: Close-up of Sally Cochran's grave.

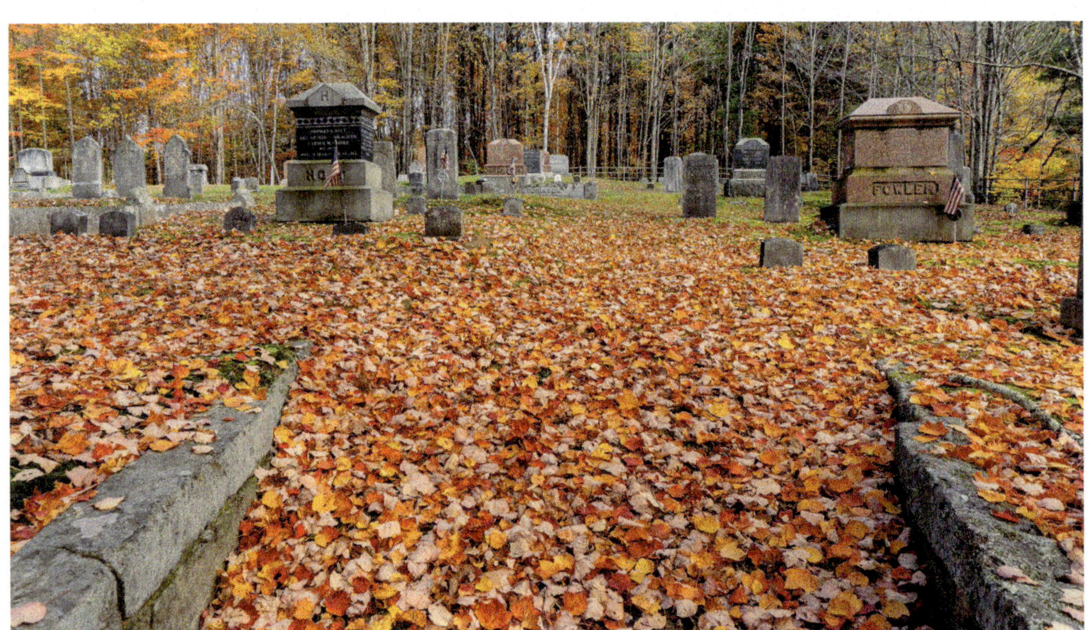

Old North Pembroke Cemetery.

9
INTERESTING GRAVES PICTURES

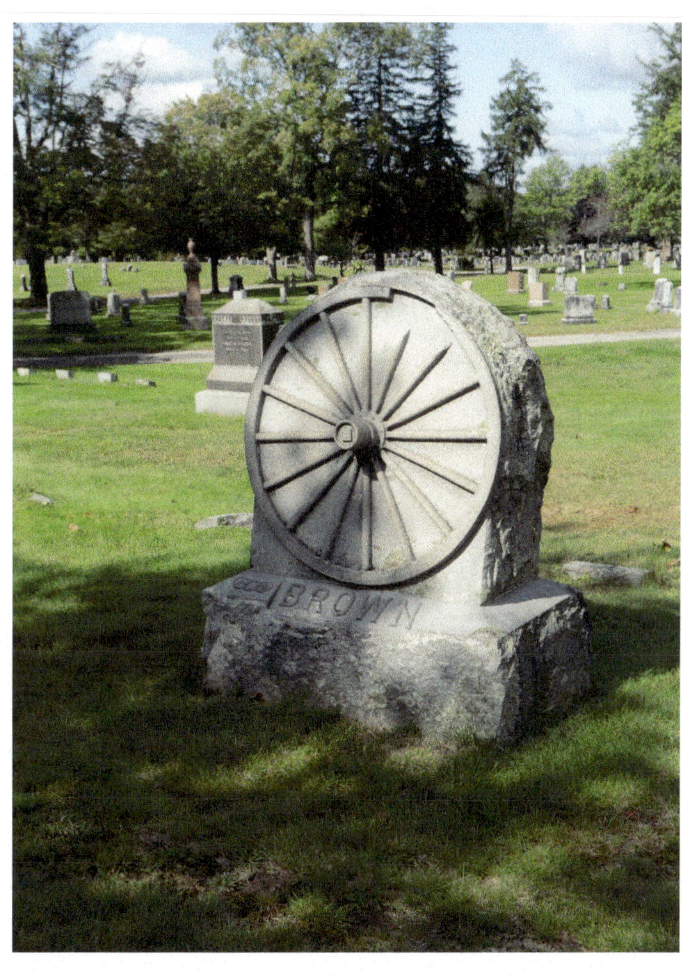

Broken Spoke, Pine Grove
Cemetery, Manchester.

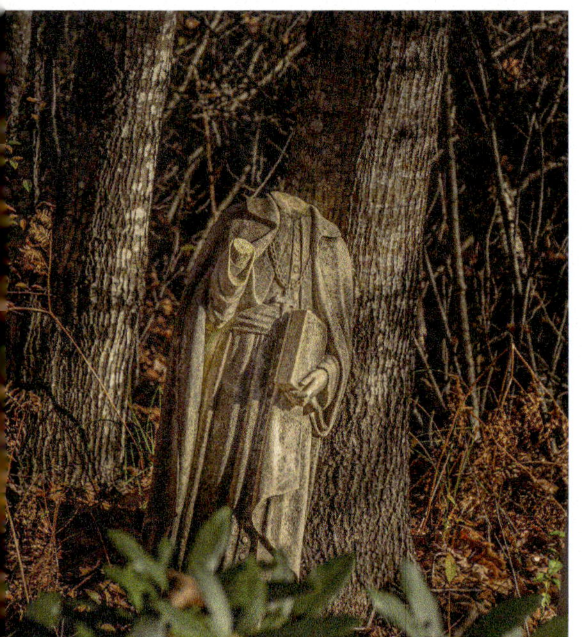

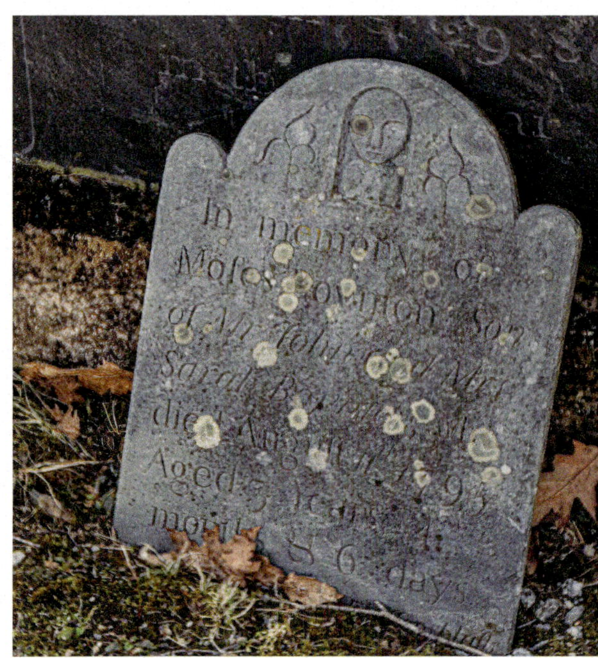

Above left: Decapitated statue rests in the swamp behind the former Laconia State School.

Above right: Died young, Nelson Cemetery.

Below left: East Cemetery, North Hampton.

Below right: Fire victims, Cotton Cemetery, Portsmouth.

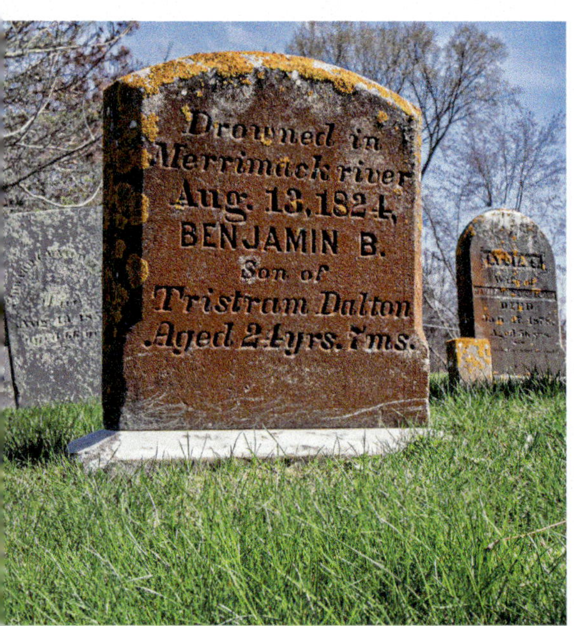

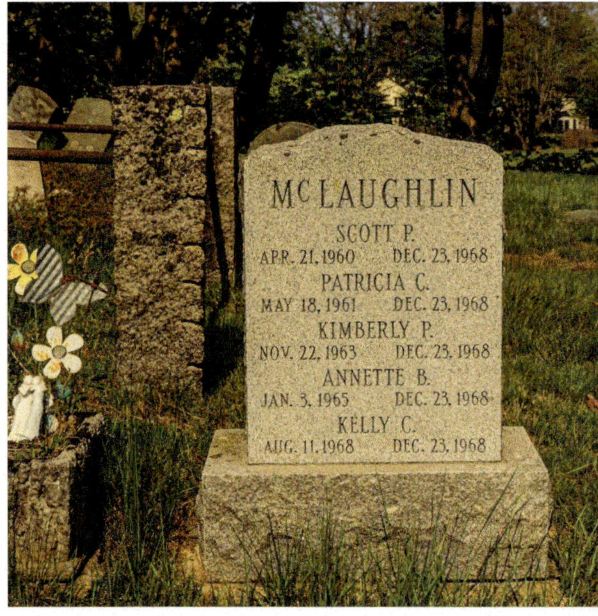

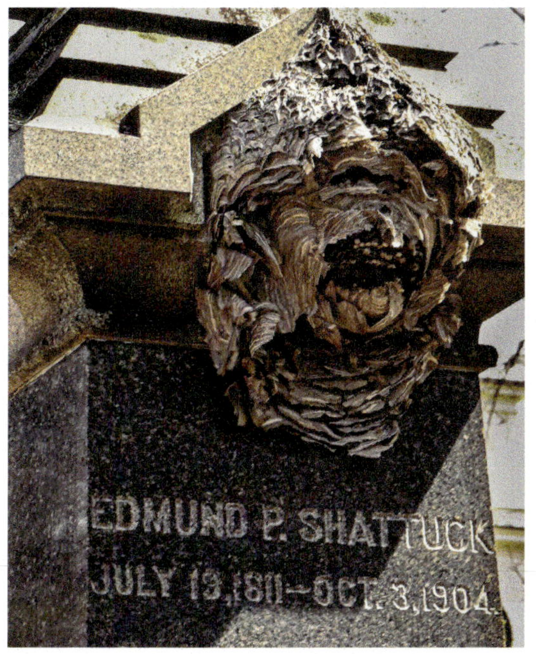

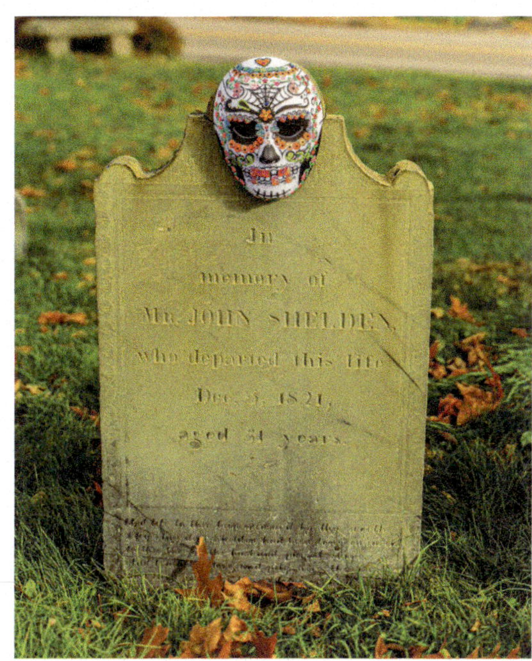

Above left: Hornets' Nest, Old Burial Ground, Jaffery.

Above right: North Cemetery, Portsmouth.

Below: North Conway Cemetery.

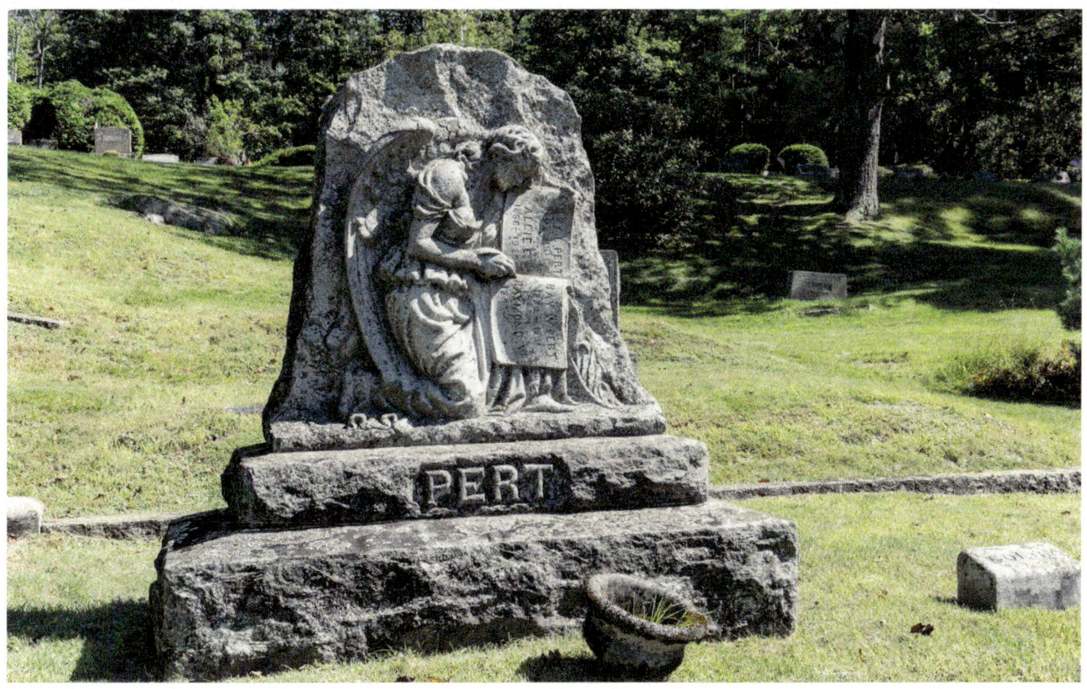

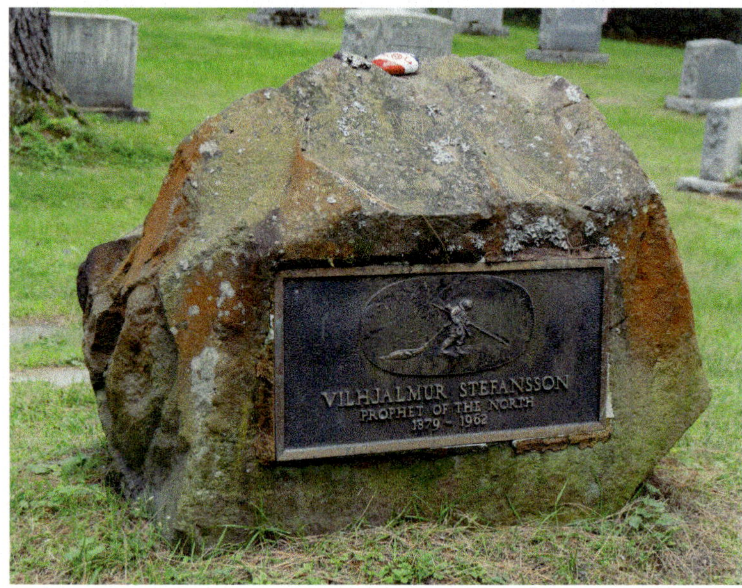

Prophet of the North,
Pine Knoll Cemetery,
Hanover.

Our books would not have been possible without the help of many great people who took the time to give us a hand along the way.

Joe Marshell, president of the Jefferson Historical Society, who provided information on Nancy Barton; Anne Clark of Clark's Bears, who allowed us to photograph the Bear Cemetery; Karla MacLeod from the Rindge Historical Society, who helped with the story of Edwin Platts; Jennifer Bretz, office manager for Facilities, Grounds, and Cemeteries for the City of Dover; Greg Paris and Jeffry Plourde from the City of Manchester Dept. of Public Works, who gave us a personal tour of Pine Grove Cemetery; Ryan O'Hora, director of the Pembroke Library, and Heather Tiddes, assistant director of the Pembroke Library, who helped with the story of Josie Langmaid; John Katwick of Milton, who helped with Joe Andrews, The Crow Indian; Cynthia Mulcahy, who helped scout out South Cemetery and locate the Glowing Stone and provided excellent editing of some of our stories; Jane Davidson, Rick's wife essential for proofreading and moral support; Bob Cottrell, Conway Public Library; Plainfield Library for finding Maxfield Parrish, Charlene Moulton Chinook Kennels information; Henry and Maureen Spenser Riverside Cemetery Tamworth information; Brian Wiggin Conway Historical Society; Sallie Macintosh sharing Shaw Brothers photos and stories; Erica McAvoy at the Moffatt-Ladd House for providing proof of Prince's Whipple's Manumission. Research has sometimes definitely included WMUR's Fritz Wetherbee, and we have given him credit. However, our heads are so full of his stories we can't always be sure which ones pointed the way to further research; we can say the same about J. Dennis Robinson of Seacoastnh.com, whose books and articles are entertaining and informative. We mention both these storytellers because they stand out when it comes to sharing New Hampshire's history with the public and we often referred to them.

Bibliography

"10th Mountain Division (United States)," Wikipedia, November 1, 2023, en.wikipedia.org/wiki/10th_Mountain_Division_(United_States)

"13 Facts about Astronaut Alan Shepard, the First American in Space," Www.mentalfloss.com, July 30, 2021, www.mentalfloss.com/article/648839/astronaut-alan-shepard-facts

"A Bibliography of New England* Gravestone Carvers," *Tomes in Progress*, July 8, 2015, winstonp.wordpress.com/new-england-graveyards/a-bibliography-of-new-england-gravestone-carvers/. Accessed November 30, 2023

"A New Hampshire Graveyard Filled with Curious Face Carvings," *Atlas Obscura*, www.atlasobscura.com/places/chester-village-cemetery. Accessed November 30, 2023

"About the Meetinghouse | Jaffrey NH," *Www.townofjaffrey.com*, www.townofjaffrey.com/about-jaffrey/pages/about-meetinghouse. Accessed November 30, 2023

"Account Suspended," *Ranger95.com*, ranger95.com/civil_war_us/officers%20of%20navy/officers8/james_s_thornton.htm. Accessed November 30, 2023

Admin, "Tommy Makem," The Music Museum of New England, November 15, 2022, www.mmone.org/tommy-makem/. Accessed December 6, 2023

"Alan Bartlett Shepard Jr. (1923–1998) - Find A..." Www.findagrave.com, www.findagrave.com/memorial/8367/alan-bartlett-shepard. Accessed November 29, 2023

"Alonzo Elliot," Wikipedia, April 23, 2022, en.wikipedia.org/wiki/Alonzo_Elliot. Accessed December 5, 2023

Archives, *L. A. Times*, "In VIP Seats, Parents Watch in Disbelief," *Los Angeles Times*, January 28, 1986, www.latimes.com/archives/la-xpm-1986-01-28-mn-773-story.html. Accessed November 30, 2023

Atkinson, N., "Alan Shepard: Complicated, Conflicted and the Consummate Astronaut," *Universe Today*, May 5, 2011, www.universetoday.com/85395/alan-shepard-complicated-conflicted-and-the-consummate-astronaut/

"'Aunt' Hannah Davis, an Inventor, Entrepreneur and Maker of Beautiful Boxes," *JCVIS*, www.jcvis.org/archives/history/aunt-hannah-davis-an-inventor-entrepreneur-and-maker-of-beautiful-boxes. Accessed December 1, 2023

"Barney and Betty Hill Incident," Wikipedia, February 13, 2023, en.wikipedia.org/wiki/Barney_and_Betty_Hill_incident

Bean, M., *Viggo Brandt-Erichsen in Jaffrey*

"Betty George," Wikipedia, October 14, 2022, en.wikipedia.org/wiki/Betty_George. Accessed December 5, 2023

"Black Mountain Resort History - New Hampshire - NewEnglandSkiHistory.com," Www.newenglandskihistory.com, www.newenglandskihistory.com/NewHampshire/blackmtn.php. Accessed December 2, 2023

"Brief History of Tamworth | Tamworth NH," Www.tamworthnh.org, www.tamworthnh.org/about-tamworth/pages/brief-history-tamworth

Brooke, L., "An Original Snowmobile," Ossipee Lake Alliance, January 15, 2009, www.ossipeelake.org/2009/01/an-original-snowmobile/. Accessed December 18, 2023

"Brooks Cemetery," *Brownfield Maine Cemeteries*, April 13, 2020, brownfieldcemeteries.com/brooks-cemetery-2/. Accessed December 2, 2023

Brown, J., "Cheswell," Cow Hampshire, www.cowhampshireblog.com/tag/cheswell/. Accessed December 5, 2023; "Downing & Abbot Company Founder and Carriage Builder of Concord New Hampshire: Lewis Downing (1792–1873)," Cow Hampshire, April 20, 2016, www.cowhampshireblog.com/2016/04/20/downing-abbott-company-founder-and-carriage-builder-of-concord-new-hampshire-lewis-downing-1792-1873/. Accessed December 27, 2023

Capt. Bancroft and the Sight of the Enemy, boston1775.blogspot.com/2014/06/capt-bancroft-and-sight-of-enemy.html. Accessed December 5, 2023

Carter, J., "The Legends behind the Gilson Road Cemetery," Anomalien.com, June 22, 2020, anomalien.com/the-legends-behind-the-gilson-road-cemetery/. Accessed November 30, 2023

Cassell, A., "This Is How a Ford Model T Became the World's First Snowmobile," HotCars, August 14, 2021, www.hotcars.com/ford-model-t-how-became-snowmobile/. Accessed December 18, 2023

Cherry, M., "Legacy of Amos Fortune Lives on in Jaffrey," WMUR, February 23, 2021, www.wmur.com/article/legacy-of-amos-fortune-lives-on-in-jaffrey/35591393. Accessed November 30, 2023

Chester Historical Society | Town of Chester, NH, Est. 1722. chesternhhistorical.org/. Accessed November 30, 2023

Clem, L., "Chinook of Wonalancet - Mt Washington Valley Vibe," Mwvvibe.com, January 29, 2020, mwvvibe.com/chinook-of-wonalancet/. Accessed November 30, 2023

Cogswell, E. C. [from old catalog, and The Library of Congress], *Memoir of the Rev. Samuel Hidden. Internet Archive* (Boston: Crocker & Brewster, 1842), archive.org/stream/memoirofrevsamue00cogs/memoirofrevsamue00cogs_djvu.txt. Accessed December 6, 2023

Conn, C., "Hannah and Her Boxes," CT Country Antiques, January 21, 2020, www.ctcountryantiques.com/post/2016/12/03/hannah-and-her-boxes. Accessed December 1, 2023

Cottrell, B., "History of Chinook Dogs |Tamworth | New Hampshire | Sledding Dogs | New England," Www.theheartofnewengland.com, www.theheartofnewengland.com/LifeInNewEngland-Chinook-Dogs.html. Accessed November 30, 2023

Cowan, N., "Sled Dog Central: Dick Moulton Remembered," Sleddogcentral.com, sleddogcentral.com/obituaries/moulton.htm. Accessed November 30, 2023

"CPT Samuel Jones Jr. (1777–1851) - Find a Grave..." Www.findagrave.com, www.findagrave.com/memorial/205277920/samuel-jones. Accessed November 30, 2023

"Cranmore Mountain Resort History - New Hampshire - NewEnglandSkiHistory.com," Www.newenglandskihistory.com, www.newenglandskihistory.com/NewHampshire/cranmore.php. Accessed December 2, 2023

Crawford, L., *Lucy Crawford's History of the White Mountains* (1978)

"CSS Alabama vs USS Kearsarge: The Greatest High Seas Duel of the Civil War," *Warfare History Network*, September 30, 2020, warfarehistorynetwork.com/article/css-alabama-vs-uss-kearsarge-the-greatest-high-seas-duel-of-the-civil-war/. Accessed November 30, 2023

Dena, "Major Savage & Old Tom, Part Two," *Big Blue Circus*, July 14, 2018, bigbluecircus.wordpress.com/2018/07/14/major-savage-old-tom-part-two/. Accessed December 5, 2023

"Did John Really Love Lucy?" *New Hampshire Magazine*, December 12, 2022, www.nhmagazine.com/did-

Dintino, M., "'The Phoenix Takes Its Rest': Visiting Woman Writer May Sarton's Grave," *Nasty Women Writers*, July 26, 2023, www.nastywomenwriters.com/the-phoenix-takes-its-rest-visiting-may-sartons-grave/. Accessed December 4, 2023

Dot, "The King's Pines," Webster Historical Society, NH, June 26, 2016, websterhistoricalsociety.org/?p=309

Eastman, T., *The History of Cranmore Mountain* (Arcadia Publishing, November 27, 2012)

Eaton, A., *Nehemiah Bean and the Amoskeag Steam Fire Engine*

"Eli Wallace Horse Cemetery in Littleton, New Hampshire - Find a Grave Cemetery," Www.

findagrave.com, www.findagrave.com/cemetery/2256977/eli-wallace-horse-cemetery. Accessed December 11, 2023

Emil Hanslin, Leading Innovator in the Housing Industry, yankeebarnhomes.com/about/history-2/. Accessed December 8, 2023

"Emil Samuel Anis Hanslin IV (1920–1987) - Find A..." Www.findagrave.com, www.findagrave.com/memorial/19460930/emil-samuel_anis-hanslin. Accessed December 8, 2023

"Ethan of the HillsTHE WHITE MOUN," Www.bartletthistory.org, www.bartletthistory.org/bartletthistory/ethanallencrawford.html. Accessed November 30, 2023

Fabrizio, R., "South Cemetery: Peaceful Present, Not-So-Restful Past," *Portsmouth Herald*, www.seacoastonline.com/story/news/2001/11/04/south-cemetery-peaceful-present-not/51298083007/. Accessed December 6, 2023

"Frank Pierce Carpenter (1845–1938) - Find a Grave..." Www.findagrave.com, www.findagrave.com/memorial/42965434/frank-pierce-carpenter. Accessed December 5, 2023

"Frank Pierce Carpenter House," Wikipedia, February 28, 2023, en.wikipedia.org/wiki/Frank_Pierce_Carpenter_House#References. Accessed December 5, 2023

"Free and Slave Populations by State (1790)," *Teaching American History*, teachingamericanhistory.org/resource/the-constitutional-convention-free-and-slave-populations-by-state-1790/

Freeman Jr, C., "Benning Wentworth," *Harvard Magazine*, November 1, 2004, www.harvardmagazine.com/2004/11/benning-wentworth.html

"Frost Cemetery Historical Marker," Www.hmdb.org, www.hmdb.org/m.asp?m=135323. Accessed November 30, 2023

"Guide to the Betty and Barney Hill Papers, 1961–2006," *Library*, October 28, 2008, library.unh.edu/find/archives/collections/betty-barney-hill-papers-1961-2006

Haag, S., "The Shaw Brothers," The Music Museum of New England, April 26, 2022, www.mmone.org/the-shaw-brothers/. Accessed December 6, 2023

Hampton's Historic "Ring" a Walking/Riding Tour of Hampton's Old Town Center

"Hannah Davis," *Historical Society of Cheshire County*, hsccnh.org/empowered-women/hannah-davis/. Accessed December 1, 2023

"Hannes Schneider - New England Ski History Biography," Newenglandskihistory.com, 2015, www.newenglandskihistory.com/biographies/schneiderhannes.php

"Harriet Patience Dame and the 2nd New Hampshire Regiment," Harriet Patience Dame and the 2nd New Hampshire Regiment, exeterhistory.blogspot.com/2012/05/harriet-patience-dame-and-2nd-new.html. Accessed December 1, 2023

"Harvey Dow Gibson," Wikipedia, September 19, 2022, en.wikipedia.org/wiki/Harvey_Dow_Gibson. Accessed December 2, 2023

Hasselgren, P.-O., "The Smallpox Epidemics in America in the 1700s and the Role of the Surgeons: Lessons to Be Learned during the Global Outbreak of COVID-19," *World Journal of Surgery*, vol. 44, no. 9, July 4, 2020, pp. 2837–2841, https://doi.org/10.1007/s00268-020-05670-4

Haven, "Decator's Place- a Malamute's Haven," decatorsplace.org/about-malamutes. Accessed November 30, 2023

"Hawks, Esther Hill," *South Carolina Encyclopedia*, www.scencyclopedia.org/sce/entries/hawks-esther-hill/

History Marker | Pittsburg New Hampshire, pittsburg-nh.com/history-marker/. Accessed December 2, 2023

"History Matters: The Sleepwalking Murder of Sally Cochran," *Portsmouth Herald*, www.seacoastonline.com/story/news/2020/07/27/history-matters-sleepwalking-murder-of-sally-cochran/113969466/. Accessed December 6, 2023

"History of Conway, New Hampshire, USA - Postcards, Stories, Ancestry, News, Travel, Photos | GREENERPASTURE," Greenerpasture.com, greenerpasture.com/Places/Details/2039. Accessed December 6, 2023

"History of Hudson, N.H. P266," www.pelhamnhhistory.org/library/pdffiles/histories/hudson/History_of_Hudson_NH_4.pdf. Accessed November 30, 2023

"History," St. John's Episcopal Church, www.stjohnsnh.org/history. Accessed December 4, 2023

History.com editors, "John Wilkes Booth," HISTORY, A&E Television Networks, August 21, 2018, www.history.com/topics/american-civil-war/john-wilkes-booth

"Home," Nashua Schoolhouse, www.nashuaschoolhouse.com/. Accessed December 5, 2023

Hounsell, J. M., *Conway, New Hampshire, 1765–1997* (Peter E. Randall Publisher, 1998)

Hudson, M., "Picking Strawberries and a Side of Mystery in Pembroke," *New Hampshire Magazine*, February 18, 2021, www.nhmagazine.com/picking-strawberries-and-a-side-of-mystery-in-pembroke/. Accessed December 6, 2023

Interpreters, Discover Power of Parks SCA, "Magnificent Tales of Metallak," NH State Parks, July 10, 2014, blog.nhstateparks.org/magnificent-tales-of-metallak/

"Jack Sharkey (1902–1994) - Find a Grave Memorial," Www.findagrave.com, www.findagrave.com/memorial/6606990/jack-. Accessed December 1, 2023

"Jack Sharkey," Southern Tier Fly Fisher, stflyfisher.wordpress.com/tag/jack-sharkey/. Accessed December 1, 2023

"Jack Sharkey," Wikipedia, Wikimedia Foundation, May 9, 2019, en.wikipedia.org/wiki/Jack_Sharkey

"Jaffrey History: Cemeteries: Phillips-Heil," Www.jaffreyhistory.org, www.jaffreyhistory.org/02places_built/05cemeteries/phillipsheil.php. Accessed November 30, 2023

"Jigger Johnson," Wikipedia, October 18, 2023, en.wikipedia.org/wiki/Jigger_Johnson. Accessed December 2, 2023

"'Jigger' Johnson | Urban Legends | Stronghold Nation," Www.stronghold-Nation.com, www.stronghold-nation.com/history/myth/jigger-johnson. Accessed December 2, 2023

"John Alfred 'English Jack' or the 'Hermit Of...'" Www.findagrave.com, www.findagrave.com/memorial/93829500/john-alfred-vials. Accessed December 5, 2023

"John Lovewell," Wikipedia, August 24, 2023, en.wikipedia.org/wiki/John_Lovewell. Accessed November 30, 2023

"John Milton Hawks," Wikipedia, November 27, 2023, en.wikipedia.org/wiki/John_Milton_Hawks. Accessed November 30, 2023

john-really-love-lucy/. Accessed December 27, 2023

Jordan, T. F., and Harold B. Lee Library, *The Jordan Memorial: Family Records of the Rev. Robert Jordan and His Descendants in America. Internet Archive* (Boston: D. Clapp & Son, 1882), archive.org/stream/jordanmemorialfa00jord/jordanmemorialfa00jord_djvu.txt. Accessed December 5, 2023

"Josiah Bartlett," National Governors Association, January 3, 2017, www.nga.org/governor/josiah-bartlett/. Accessed December 4, 2023

"Josiah Bartlett," Thefamouspeople.com, 2011, www.thefamouspeople.com/profiles/josiah-bartlett-3929.php

"Josiah Bartlett," Wikipedia, September 23, 2022, en.wikipedia.org/wiki/Josiah_Bartlett

Kayworth, A. E., and Potvin, R. G., *The Scalp Hunters: Abenaki Ambush at Lovewell Pond, 1725* (Boston: Branden Books, 2002)

Kelly, G., "The History of Peyton Place in Gilmanton NH," *New Hampshire Magazine*, March 1, 2013, www.nhmagazine.com/50-shades-of-grace/

Landrigan, L., "Wentworth Cheswell, the Black Man Who Rode with Revere," New England Historical Society, January 1, 2017, newenglandhistoricalsociety.com/wentworth-cheswell-black-man-rode-paul-revere/

"Lewis Downing Conquers the West with the Concord Coach," *New England Historical Society*, November 23, 2013, newenglandhistoricalsociety.com/lewis-downing-conquers-west-concord-coach/. Accessed December 27, 2023

"Lewis Downing Sr. (1792–1873) - Find a Grave..." Www.findagrave.com, www.findagrave.com/memorial/113733751/lewis-downing. Accessed December 27, 2023

"Life and Death in Early Hampton: Tour of Pine Grove Cemetery," *Portsmouth Herald*, www.seacoastonline.com/story/news/2021/07/06/life-and-death-early-hampton-nh-tour-pine-grove-cemetery/7875007002/. Accessed December 4, 2023

Life of Amos Fortune | the Amos Fortune Forum. amosfortune.com/life-of-amos-fortune/

Liu, M., "Robert Lowell at 100: Why His Poetry Has Never Been More Relevant," *The Guardian*, March 1, 2017, www.theguardian.com/books/booksblog/2017/mar/01/robert-lowell-at-100-poetry-centenary

"Longfellow: The Battle of Lovell's Pond, Portland Gazette," HENRY WADSWORTH LONGFELLOW, www.hwlongfellow.org/poems_poem.php?pid=2095. Accessed November 30, 2023

"Lucy Lambert Hale," Wikipedia, August 20, 2020, en.wikipedia.org/wiki/Lucy_Lambert_Hale

"Luther Parker," *BaladoDécouverte*, baladodecouverte.com/circuits/356/poi/9067/luther-parker. Accessed December 2, 2023

"Matthew Thornton (1713–1803) | WikiTree FREE Family Tree," Www.wikitree.com, www.wikitree.com/wiki/Thornton-1562. Accessed December 4, 2023

Matthew Thornton | Descendants of the Signers of the Declaration of Independence, www.dsdi1776.com/signer/matthew-thornton/

"Matthew Thornton," Wikipedia, October 31, 2023, en.wikipedia.org/wiki/Matthew_Thornton. Accessed December 4, 2023

"May Sarton (1912–1995) - Find a Grave Memorial," Www.findagrave.com, www.findagrave.com/memorial/1222/may-sarton. Accessed December 4, 2023

"May Sarton," Wikipedia, January 6, 2023, en.wikipedia.org/wiki/May_Sarton

Metallak His Legacy (Colebrook, NH: Leibl Printing)

"Metallak," Wikipedia, November 11, 2021, en.wikipedia.org/wiki/Metallak

Metallak's Life. Prince of Darkness (A.D. Noyes, 1992)

Metmuseum.org, 2020, www.metmuseum.org/toah/hd/astg/hd_astg.htm

Milbouer, S., *et al.*, "A New Hampshire Graveyard Foliage Tour," *New Hampshire Magazine*, October 1, 2023, www.nhmagazine.com/graveyard-fall-foliage-tour/. Accessed November 30, 2023

Monahan '29, R. S. "LUCY CRAWFORD'S HISTORY of the WHITE MOUNTAINS. | Dartmouth Alumni Magazine | DECEMBER 1966," *Dartmouth Alumni Magazine | the Complete Archive*, archive.dartmouthalumnimagazine.com/article/1966/12/1/lucy-crawfords-history-of-the-white-mountains

"Monandock Moments No. 35: Samuel Jones' Leg," Historical Society of Cheshire County, hsccnh.org/education/resources/monadnock-moments/item/monandock-moments-no-35-samuel-jones-leg/. Accessed November 30, 2023

"Mosses from an Old Manse/Roger Malvin's Burial - Wikisource, the Free Online Library," Wikisource.org, 2022, en.wikisource.org/wiki/Mosses_from_an_Old_Manse/Roger_Malvin%27s_Burial. Accessed November 30, 2023

Mystery, Legends Surround Gilson Cemetery | News, Sports, Jobs - the Cabinet Press, www.cabinet.com/news/hb-news/2013/10/24/mystery-legends-surround-gilson-cemetery/

Nast, C., "Grace Metalious: Peyton Place's Real Victim," *Vanity Fair*, January 22, 2007, www.vanityfair.com/news/2006/03/peytonplace200603

neskimuse, "The Ski History of Bartlett, New Hampshire," New England Ski Museum, May 30, 2005, newenglandskimuseum.org/the-ski-history-of-bartlett-new-hampshire/. Accessed December 2, 2023

"New Hampshire Historical Society - Harriet Dame: New Hampshire's Angel of Mercy," Nhhistory.org, 2015, www.nhhistory.org/Research/Online-Exhibitions/Collection

"New Hampshire: A Tale of Two (or More) Kearsarge," *Cow Hampshire*, September 5, 2006, www.cowhampshireblog.com/2006/09/05/new-hampshire-a-tale-of-two-or-more-kearsarge/. Accessed November 30, 2023

"New Hampshire's 19th Century Independent Nation-State," *Atlas Obscura*, www.atlasobscura.com/places/republic-of-indian-stream

"North Barnstead New Hampshire's Harriet P. Dame: The "Florence Nightingale" of the Civil War (1815–1900)," *Cow Hampshire*, November 11, 2007, www.cowhampshireblog.com/2007/11/11/north-barnstead-new-hampshires-harriet-p-dame-the-florence-nightingale-of-the-civil-war-1815-1900/. Accessed December 1, 2023

"North Cemetery," City of Portsmouth, www.cityofportsmouth.com/city/north-cemetery. Accessed December 4, 2023

Ocker, J. W., "Upon This Rock," *New Hampshire Magazine*, December 4, 2020, www.nhmagazine.com/upon-this-rock/. Accessed December 6, 2023

"Officials Solve Mystery about the Human Skull and the Littleton Horse Cemetery - More or Less," New Hampshire Public Radio, January 12, 2012, www.nhpr.org/north-country/2012-01-12/officials-solve-mystery-about-the-human-skull-and-the-littleton-horse-cemetery-more-or-less. Accessed December 11, 2023

"Old Burial Ground Walking Tour," Old Burial Ground Walking Tour, JAFFREY HISTORICAL

SOCIET y, www.jaffreyhistory.org/11events/obgtour.pdf

"Old Street Cemetery in Peterborough, New Hampshire - Find a Grave Cemetery," Www. findagrave.com, www.findagrave.com/cemetery/1973327/old-street-cemetery. Accessed December 5, 2023

"Old Tom the Horse (Unknown-1885) - Find a Grave..." Www.findagrave.com, www.findagrave. com/memorial/56227265/old_tom-the_horse. Accessed December 5, 2023

"Ordination Rock - Tamworth, NH, USA - Citizen Memorials on Waymarking.com," Www. waymarking.com, www.waymarking.com/waymarks/WMECHV_Ordination_Rock_ Tamworth_NH_USA. Accessed December 6, 2023

"Our Town," Peterborough Players, www.peterboroughplayers.org/our-town.html. Accessed December 5, 2023

Paradis, S., "South Street Cemetery Has Its Share of Ghosts," www.seanparadis.com/ghosts-of-south-street-cemetery/. Accessed December 4, 2023

Peek, J., "Rare 1926 Ford Model T Snowmobile Has the White Stuff," Hagerty Media, February 5, 2021, www.hagerty.com/media/automotive-history/rare-1926-ford-model-t-snowmobile-has-the-white-stuff/. Accessed December 18, 2023

"PETERBOROUGH PLAYERS PRESENT OUR TOWN, DOWNTOWN, in OUR TOWN with GORDON CLAPP," Peterborough Players, www.peterboroughplayers.org/news/peterborough-players-present-our-town-downtown-in-our-town-with-gordon-clapp. Accessed December 5, 2023

"Pine Grove Cemetery Walking Tour 9/25/2017," Www.youtube.com, www.youtube.com/watch?v=HJF61qNQQXY&t=154s. Accessed December 5, 2023

Poetry Foundation, "May Sarton," November 23, 2021, www.poetryfoundation.org/poets/may-sarton

"Poetry Foundation," *Poetry Foundation*, 2013, www.poetryfoundation.org/poets/robert-lowell

"Point of Graves Burial Ground," Wikipedia, March 29, 2021, en.wikipedia.org/wiki/Point_of_Graves_Burial_Ground

"Point of Graves Historical Marker," Www.hmdb.org, www.hmdb.org/m.asp?m=76581

Prescott, A., *et al.*, *Report of the Trial of Abraham Prescott, for the Murder of Mrs. Sally Cochran of Pembroke, June 23, 1833: Executed at Hopkinton, January 6, 1836*, internet archive (Manchester, N.H.: Daily Mirror, 1869), archive.org/details/reportoftrialofa1869pres/page/12/mode/2up. Accessed December 6, 2023

"Quotes by May Sarton," *Literary Ladies Guide*, October 6, 2017, www.literaryladiesguide.com/author-quotes/quotes-may-sarton/

"Radio Field Trip: Exploring Portsmouth's Haunted History," New Hampshire Public Radio, October 31, 2018, www.nhpr.org/nh-news/2018-10-31/radio-field-trip-exploring-portsmouths-haunted-history. Accessed December 7, 2023

"Republic of Indian Stream," Wikipedia, November 26, 2022, en.wikipedia.org/wiki/Republic_of_Indian_Stream

"Rev Fr Robert Jordan (1611–1679) - Find a Grave..." Www.findagrave.com, www.findagrave. com/memorial/104730781/robert-jordan. Accessed December 5, 2023

"Revolutionary Graves of New Hampshire NAME BORN PLACE of BIRTH DIED PLACE of DEATH MARRIED FATHER BURIED TOWN CEMETERY OCCUPATION SERVICE PENSION SOURCE," 1750

"Roads to the Great War: The Buddies Memorial of Jaffrey, New Hampshire," Roads to the Great War, May 14, 2017, roadstothegreatwar-ww1.blogspot.com/2017/05/jaffrey-new-hampshires-buddies-memorial.html. Accessed December 1, 2023

"Robert Lowell," Wikipedia, December 30, 2020, en.wikipedia.org/wiki/Robert_Lowell

Robinson, J. D., *Mystery on the Isles of Shoals* (Simon and Schuster, November 18, 2014)

Rojo, H. W., "Nutfield Genealogy: Tombstone Tuesday ~ Abolitionists and Doctors, Husband and Wife, Esther and John Hawks of Manchester, New Hampshire," Nutfield Genealogy, June 17, 2014, nutfieldgenealogy.blogspot.com/2014/06/tombstone-tuesday-abolitionists-and.html. Accessed November 30, 2023

ScenicNH Photography, LLC and Erin Paul Donovan, "Presidential Range, New Hampshire - Random History," July 30, 2019, www.scenicnh.com/blog/2019/07/presidential-range-history/; "Presidential Range, New Hampshire - Random History," July 30, 2019, www.scenicnh.com/

blog/2019/07/presidential-range-history/. Accessed November 30, 2023

"Signers of the Declaration of Independence: Josiah Bartlett," Www.ushistory.org, www.ushistory.org/declaration/signers/bartlett.html

"Smallpox Cemetery History | Jaffrey NH," Www.townofjaffrey.com, www.townofjaffrey.com/cemetery/pages/smallpox-cemetery-history. Accessed December 4, 2023.

"Snowmobile," Wikipedia, Wikimedia Foundation, April 3, 2019, en.wikipedia.org/wiki/Snowmobile

Speare, E. A., *Stories of New Hampshire*, October 1, 1976

"Stagecoach," Www.rottentomatoes.com, www.rottentomatoes.com/m/1019774-stagecoach

"Suncook Town Tragedy - Mabel Wilson Tatro (Two Versions)," Www.youtube.com, www.youtube.com/watch?v=-6QuB3rLtbM. Accessed December 1, 2023

"Tammy Grimes – Biography," IMDb, www.imdb.com/name/nm0342245/bio/. Accessed December 6, 2023

"Tammy Grimes (1934–2016) - Find a Grave Memorial," Www.findagrave.com, www.findagrave.com/memorial/172046028/tammy-grimes#:~:text=Find%20a%20Grave%2C%20database%20en%20afbeeldingen%20%28https%3A%2F%2Fnl.findagrave.com%2Fmemorial%2F172046028%2Ftammy-grimes%3A%20geopend%29%2C. Accessed December 6, 2023

"Tammy Grimes," Wikipedia, November 27, 2023, en.wikipedia.org/wiki/Tammy_Grimes. Accessed December 6, 2023

Thaxter, C., "A Memorable Murder," *The Atlantic*, May 1, 1875, www.theatlantic.com/magazine/archive/1875/05/a-memorable-murder/631038/1873. Accessed December 6, 2023

The Associated Press, "New Historical Marker in New Hampshire Notes Former Slave Who Became Town's Nurse," WMUR, January 18, 2023, www.wmur.com/article/barrington-new-hampshire-benjamin-balch-aggie/42537112. Accessed December 7, 2023

"The Chinook Trail | Tamworth | New Hampshire," Www.theheartofnewengland.com, www.theheartofnewengland.com/LifeInNewEngland-Chinook-Trail.html. Accessed November 30, 2023

"The Elusive Trail of Lucy Hale," Www.seacoastnh.com, www.seacoastnh.com/History/History-Matters/The-Elusive-Trail-of-Lucy-Hale/. Accessed December 27, 2023

"The Elusive Trail of Lucy Hale," *Www.seacoastnh.com*, www.seacoastnh.com/the-elusive-trail-of-lucy-hale/?start=3. Accessed December 27, 2023

"The Grave of a Severed Leg," *Atlas Obscura*, www.atlasobscura.com/places/captain-jones-leg-grave. Accessed November 30, 2023

The History of Cranmore Mountain (Charleston, SC: History Press, 2012)

"The Model T Ford Snowmobile Club - Brief History," Modeltfordsnowmobile.com, modeltfordsnowmobile.com/LCmainBriefHistory.htm. Accessed December 18, 2023

"The Republic of Indian Stream (1832–1835)," *Big Think*, bigthink.com/strange-maps/27-the-republic-of-indian-stream-1832-1835/

"The Somnambulism Defense: The Sleepwalking Murderer of Pembroke, N.H.," *New England Historical Society*, June 5, 2017, newenglandhistoricalsociety.com/somnambulism-defense-sleepwalking-murderer-pembroke/. Accessed December 6, 2023

"They Liked to Teach the World to Sing: The Shaw Brothers' N.H. Folk Legacy," New Hampshire Public Radio, June 14, 2018, www.nhpr.org/arts-culture/2018-06-14/they-liked-to-teach-the-world-to-sing-the-shaw-brothers-n-h-folk-legacy. Accessed December 6, 2023

"Thornton, James S.," Public2.Nhhcaws.local, www.history.navy.mil/our-collections/photography/us-people/t/thornton-james-s.html#:~:text=In%20April%201863%20he%20became. Accessed November 30, 2023

"Tommy Makem (1932–2007) - Find a Grave Memorial," Www.findagrave.com, www.findagrave.com/memorial/20747498/tommy-makem. Accessed December 6, 2023

"Tommy Makem," Wikipedia, December 2, 2023, en.wikipedia.org/wiki/Tommy_Makem. Accessed December 6, 2023

"Wentworth Cheswell (1746–1817) - Find a Grave...," Www.findagrave.com, www.findagrave.com/memorial/6836262/wentworth-cheswell. Accessed December 5, 2023

West, B., "West in New England: SONG of LOVEWELL'S FIGHT," West in New England, October 3, 2015, westinnewengland.blogspot.com/2015/10/song-of-lovewells-fight.html.

Accessed November 30, 2023

Wetherbee, F., *Fritz: More Stories from New Hampshire Chronicle* (Concord, N.H.: Plaidswede, 2007)

"White Mountain Chronicles: Jigger Johnson, the Last Woodsman," *The Conway Daily Sun*, May 26, 2017, www.conwaydailysun.com/news/white-mountain-chronicles-jigger-johnson-the-last-woodsman/article_0533ca81-509e-5ca9-a80c-4c6190a579ea.html. Accessed December 2, 2023.

"Who Was Alan Shepard? (Grades K-4) – NASA," May 11, 2011, www.nasa.gov/learning-resources/for-kids-and-students/who-was-alan-shepard-grades-k-4/

Wikipedia Contributors, "Alan Shepard," Wikipedia, Wikimedia Foundation, September 24, 2019, en.wikipedia.org/wiki/Alan_Shepard

Writer, Staff, "Snowmobiles — a N.H. Original," *Foster's Daily Democrat*, www.fosters.com/story/lifestyle/2010/07/08/snowmobiles-8212-n-h-original/51547707007/. Accessed December 18, 2023

www.bibliopolis.com, "Abr'm Prescott's Confession of the Murder of Mrs. Sally Cochran. By Broadside, Murder, Private Individual at the Bar on the Lawbook Exchange, Ltd," The Lawbook Exchange, Ltd., www.lawbookexchange.com/pages/books/66538/broadside-murder-private-individual-at-the-bar/abrm-prescotts-confession-of-the-murder-of-mrs-sally-cochran. Accessed December 6, 2023

"You Asked, We Answered: What's the Story behind That Mysterious Gravestone in New Boston?" New Hampshire Public Radio, March 9, 2018, www.nhpr.org/nh-news/2018-03-09/you-asked-we-answered-whats-the-story-behind-that-mysterious-gravestone-in-new-boston. Accessed December 4, 2023

Zwicker, R. J., *New Hampshire Book of the Dead* (The History Press, 2012)